Exit isA safe Place

National Library of Canada Cataloguing
in Publication

Hamilton, Corey
    Exit Is A Safe Place/Corey Hamilton

Poems.
ISBN 0-9697305-4-3

All Photography © 2005 Corey Hamilton
Except Middle Photograph On Back
© 2005 Larry Hamilton
Design/Layout by Corey Hamilton

First Printing

Published by Dramatic Situations
            P.O. Box 696
            Edmonton, AB
            T5J 2L4
            CANADA
www.dramaticsituations.com

Exit is a Safe Place

Corey Hamilton

THE REPLACEMENT PARTS
ARE NOT FREE

Let's do some homework
Together
While images of
Me at age ten
Watching my
Grandfather and
Another man talk
To each other

The other man
Is draining the truck
Of my grandfather's life
I let the wheat
Run over and in between
My fingers
I catch a handful
And open my hand

To let it run out
And in between
My fingers
I do this again
But this time
I keep the wheat
I look at it a bit
And bit by bit

I eat all of the wheat
I chew all of the
Small buds and swallow

The taste in my mouth
The smell of my hands
It left an impression
On me then
And even now

And now the smell
The taste the sound
Of the wheat
Pouring out of that truck
Just like my concentration
On my duties and work
All those old scenes
Of simplicity and tranquillity

Are worth more to me now
Than they were
To me then
They have faded somewhat
I can't really smell
Or taste that dry dusty texture
But I felt it and still do feel it
And even though I have

Been in more sterilised cold
Rooms doing jobs, homework
They can never even
Come close to replacing those past memories

William Ronald Hamilton was born on January 19th, 1915 in Rossburn Manitoba. To family and friends he was known as "Ron" due to the fact that his first and middle name were mistakenly reversed on his birth certificate. I knew him as Grandpa Hamilton, my father's father. Grandpa Hamilton and his wife, Mary Black were two of the most important people in my life. My reasoning behind this will follow.

One of the earliest memories I have involving my Grandfather is from when I was five or six. I was playing with some toys, as were my two sisters, in the living room of my Grandparent's farmhouse in Rossburn. Suddenly my Aunt Judy, the youngest of my father's four siblings, came running through the living room screaming to call the hospital. Apparently my Grandfather got bucked off of the horse he and my Aunt owned. He ended up getting the wind knocked out of him and breaking a few ribs. Even though he healed okay, it was quite a scare for everyone involved.

This last incident happened on one of the many summers my family and I spent at the farm. We tried to spend as much time with my Grandparents for around 1976 my Grandfather was diagnosed with cancer. No one admitted it at the time, but in the back of our heads, we thought Grandpa may lose the battle. So it may have been an unconscious decision to spend as much time with him as possible. The fact that almost everyone over the age of 60 on my father's side of the family has had or died from cancer was not reassuring.

For me personally most of my memories of Grandpa were good. I used to wake up early all of the time at the farm when I was younger and dress as soon as I could and waited for Grandpa to say, "Let's go for a walk." We would walk for awhile around his farm until he figured that it was time for breakfast. Almost always Grandpa would start a food fight.

This usually meant more work for Grandma. My Grandpa was a very demanding man, but Grandma always put up with it.

In addition to Grandpa being demanding, so was I, and to certain degree I still am. My mother feels that I got this trait from him. My mother and Grandpa locked horns on many occasions, but that's for another essay.

I understand that this is, for the most part, not very organised, but I believe that memories are almost never organised. With that in mind, I will go back to those early morning walks with Grandpa. He never said much unless I asked him a question. I remember once when I was about 17 I wondered aloud which Prime Minister candidate I would vote for when I was 18. Grandpa said, "It's too big." I didn't understand. He elaborated, explaining that things really don't change that much when they are that big. He also said that I should worry more about it at a local level and let the chips fall where they may federally. I thought this was quite profound for just a "rural redneck." There were also other bits of food for thought, like: don't complain, work it out and live one day at a time. Granted they weren't the most original pieces of information but they meant, and still do mean, a lot to me.

Grandpa taught me to be honest, fair, realistic and to try and always have fun. He never drank alcohol, smoked, did drugs or even swore.

Fun was almost mandatory with Grandpa around. Like aforementioned food fights, there were water fights and loads of practical jokes. Let me set up a scene for you: my grandparents had lots of animals like cows, horses and even a goat. The most common animals were cats, and boy were they wild. I was about 14 and Grandpa, Dad and I were watching the cats and kittens eat the scraps of food I had put out for them. The largest cat had its' back to me while it was eating and Grandpa told me to pick it up. Luckily it was winter and I had my big leather gloves on because that cat, which was not domesticated, would have torn my hands to pieces. As it was I ended up with perforated gloves. Grandpa and Dad laughed heartily. I laughed hesitantly.

It is hard to sum up what Grandpa meant to me with all of the fading memories, but I will try my best to explain further. There was a bit of a generation gap between us. My almost severe interest in judo, hockey, art, poetry and music stirred almost nothing in my Grandpa. Even when I went through my punk rock phase and other childish rebelliousness, Grandpa (and even Grandma, which is why she is still so important to me) never made fun of me or were never disrespectful to me, unlike some of my family, close or distant. There was one incident where Grandpa hit me extremely hard. Looking back, I hold no grudges because I did something he told me not to do. I told my Dad this and he was shocked. Dad was scared to tell me because he thought it may skew my opinion of him, but Grandpa was always stressed out and very intense. Probably because he had to support five kids and a wife on a shoe string budget. The level of intensity was so bad that Dad could hardly wait to graduate from high school so he could move out. Dad went on to say that as intimidating as his six foot one, two hundred and thirty pound father was, he never raised a hand to his children. I still see Grandpa as a sometimes serious, big teddy bear.

Of all of the differences between Grandpa and myself we had one thing in common. We loved baseball. So almost every summer when the whole family gathered at the farm, we would always play some ball in the farm yard. My fondest memory was Grandpa hitting an underhand pitch so hard that it went from one end of the yard to the other and even cleared the roof of the barn. At 74, Grandpa couldn't run very well but this time he didn't need to.

This was the second last time I saw Grandpa before

I saw him in the hospital. I will not go into my feelings about seeing him naked except for a special undergarment so he could urinate, for the cancer was eating his body. I will try to forget how much weight he lost in the last months of his life and the pain and the open sores and the chemotherapy. Hearing the stories of his pain, hallucinations and going from 230 pounds to 150 pounds in a span of a couple of months. This has caused my views to be extremely polarised so that if I had to choose between cancer or A.I.D.S. to die from, I would choose A.I.D.S. in a second. I will block it all out by thinking about that rocket of a baseball he hit landing somewhere in the pasture behind the barn.

William Ronald Hamilton died March 12, 1990, losing a 13 year battle to cancer. My only regret about Grandpa and my relationship is that in our final meeting in the hospital in early 1990, I never told him that I loved him. It took me almost four years to deal with his death, I just hope that he somehow knows that I loved him, still do love him and that I miss him very much.

MOST SUBMERGED

Sometimes when I wake
I feel as if somebody
Is dragging me
Pulling me up and out of
The bottom of a lake
Where I am resting
Submerged in the silt

I am being pulled up
Out to the surface
Whether I like it or not
The water is green
Dark and murky
I am being dragged up
To all the brightness

Whether I like it or not
I am being pulled up
And out and above the surface
Where all the brightness is
All the noise and commotion is
Sometimes I really wish
I could stay asleep like this forever

BARE NECESSITIES

I picture myself
Drinking a coke
While walking
In a mall
And while swallowing
I run into someone
Who reminds me of you
Maybe it's a coincidence
Or maybe she's a cousin of yours
I start to choke
And cough some
The woman notices
My discomfort some
And would say something like
"What's your problem?"
And I would reply back
"Nothing, I just thought
You looked like someone
I thought I knew"
And she would
Just look away
And I would
Just stand there
Trying to swallow
But not being able to
Because the woman
Really was you

NORMAL DREAM

I hate dreaming about school
In the dream last night
Everyone asked me what
I was doing
Just trying to do like everyone else
But it still came to the same
There's a punk punk him
Punch him in his mind
In it I was touching
A female intimately
She was on top of me
It was a display
For everyone else to think
I was just normal
I couldn't wait for it to end
People say I guess I was
Normal for awhile
The song I was supposed to hear
Was "Beat Me Senseless"
By the Circle Jerks
I hate dreaming about school
There's no line in that song
That says there's a punk
Punk him
It was a display
Normal for awhile
I hate dreaming about school

PASSING WIND

Field of joy
Flesh of yesterday
Like watching
Some female I don't know
Masturbate for reasons
I don't know
I don't want to see that
Do you read me
Do you read me
Go away
I'm going away
It's none of my business
So I'm learning
To go away
In the meantime
Field of joy
Mean of time
Flesh of yesterday
You're in the opposite lane
And to think that
If one minute passed
I would be more than half way done
Free this
Free that
I don't know
Why
Can't I
I can't get enough of this clip
I'd like to touch
The small of her back
Where all the skin

Looks so smooth and white
Is that so unusual
Is that so unusual?
But when and where
Will you draw the line
Is
Is the glass of water
Half full
Or half empty
Or both
When and where
Will I draw the line
I try to think
When I last felt this way
But it makes me feel guilty

CUSTODIAL TREATMENT

Art
Mr. Bergmann
You both helped me
Before
Can you help me now
I know I've
Asked a lot
In the past
But I need
Just one more
Favour
I'm giving her
Just another week
It will be the
Longest week
In my life
I need something
To make the time
Pass quicker than a
Snail's pace
I can't take it
Any more
The paintings
Your music
It all helped me
Then
Can it help me
Now
Then and now
Then and now
I didn't have to

Say anything to her
But I did anyways
Now look at the
Reaction I got
I've always felt
That I didn't
Have to say
Anything to you
But I did anyways
And now look at the
Reaction I got
And look how
Easily the time passed
Well more easily
Than it did
Before I asked you
Someone said
The art and
Mr. Bergmann
Are like putting
A bandaid
Over a gunshot wound
I'd like to think
That you're what
Causes the wound
To start knitting
Itself back together
And I'm the one
Who does the rest
I'll stand
In front of the paintings
And listen
To your songs
When I've finished
This notebook

COIL

Wrapping around my skull
Wading in my obscenities
Crunching my buds under foot
Spinning and wrapping
All around me now
Just because of a sparkle
In my eye
In my eyes
Possibilities are there
But chances are slow
The heat is being shut off
The heat was shut off
Long long ago
And now the weeds
Of my own fears are
Wrapping around my skull

OPEN THAT CLOSED WINDOW

Here we go
Here we go again
I don't want you bowing at me
I'm not worth it
No music will help me
I'm never going to mail
Anything anymore
All over again
All over again
Why write it's
Never right anyways
Why read
I can't read
It right anyways
Where's all that pressure
And why can't
I write when I'm happy
There's that twitch again
Twitch all over this paper
What's the use
I hate saying that
I push my strength
To the limits writing
More free time
Than is healthy
Why are some people not
Considered to be habitants
Language is the only
Barrier there, but
Isn't it always.

VIEW IGNORANT

Your name runs
Like molten lead
Off of my tongue
Through, in and under
My opinion
Yes
That's almost all
I can say
Until I'm big and
Strong again

NUMBER FOUR

It's a deeper shade of brown
Sitting around a table
Full of intelligence
And I'm at the other end
Other end of the spectrum
Other end of myself
Other end with myself
Shhh, I say to myself
Let the brightness talk
I can't speak of much
More than curtains and toys
No river to me just a stream
And I am number four

JUST EVEN

Just even
Even it out
Even with me
Calluses won't let
Me alone
Calluses have
Never been
Don't open
That door
Just to scare
Me
Just me
Because I am
Scared enough
As it is
As it's just even
Even with me
Just me
Just even

CHAIN DREAMS

I care not of your past
Unless it incinerates
Your future
But I'd like to see you
Prove that sort of pregnancy
In your chained up
Shackled down castle
There is nothing relevant
In my size anymore

It's just like mailboxes
Attached to a post
Waiting to be filled
Looking like some sort of
Group of brightly coloured
Barnacles growing on a post
With guitar strings
For spider webs all over
To show age

Both of us
Both of our stories
Are so old and
Unconnected in any way
It was all in my head
To think they were
Connected
I am a dreamer of
Things that will never come

I am not
Nothing
I am not
Nothing
I am not
I don't want
To be examined
Or run on
I am
Dying
I am drunk
On my own
Feelings of
Worthlessness
And of being
Used
And talked down
I am not
Nothing
Hardly
When I feel
Just that
Just like that

THE FLOWER

Picture this. If you can.

A flower. One of millions but only one of its kind that you can see for miles and miles. A flower. With a long slender stem. The stem is a deep, mossy green and it's slightly woody too. It is woody with long thick roots. Roots to feed it and nourish it. The woody stem, the long thick roots are all there because of its life. The flower's past life. The flower's past lives. The generations of this one flower are many. Countless. The changes have occurred slowly and subtly.

The long thick roots go deep into the soil, for this flower has seen just as many dry seasons, as it has wet seasons. The stem has become woody and strong with tiny thorns to keep would be predators away. The strong stem has come about because of the unpredictable elements. The stem is able to withstand howling winds, as well as a heavy down pour of rain. The flower has small leaves at the top of the stem, to absorb more light for nourishment. The flower, over a period of eons, has been forced to adapt to its surroundings. It has done very well, for here it stands, like a message to its past relatives. "Here I am! Here I am! I live! Your past experiences have made me strong!" it cries out. A beacon saying that all was not when they died.

Yet in mentioning all of these strengths of the flower we have forgotten the one thing that makes it unique. The one trait that makes it one in the same as the ones who died before it was born.

The flower itself.

The flower itself. The petals. The petals of this one flower are the same as the petals of the generations before. They are shaped like a child's hands, when they cup them together to catch some water. In addition to this, the petals are the most magnificent colour of purple you have ever seen. Not magenta, not even royal purple. Just purple, a pure, deep purple that makes you want to go up to the flower and stroke it lightly with you finger tips. Go on, pet the petals gently. See how soft they are, it's like petting air that's firm or stroking a newborn baby's hair. You can feel something is there, but the petals are so soft that you have to look and make sure that your fingers haven't been deceived.

You bring your fingers to your nose and sniff lightly. Your nose experiences one of the most beautiful smells ever. It's almost intoxicating, the sweetness and strength of the scent. Isn't it amazing!

So you stand back and just take it all in. The roots that feed the stem. The stem that supports the leaves and the petals. Incredible, all of this working together to keep its beauty alive.

You have been so astounded by this flower's splendour that you have failed to notice that nearby is another flower.

The second flower is a bit uphill from the purple flower and is quite different from the purple flower. The second flower is a distinct yellow, like the sun. So it is quite different, but pretty anyways. In addition to this there are several more yellow flowers scattered all over the horizon.

Each flower has been has been doing their own individual movements to live for some time now. You wonder how long they have lived so near one another and if they know how different they are from each other.

You feel a slight breeze and realise that it is time for mother nature to play its part in the flower's lives. The purple flower is downwind from the yellow flower and it is pollinated by the yellow's pollen. You watch as a little time passes and you notice the yellow flower starting to fade and die. You've also noticed that most of the older yellow flowers have all died and are being replaced by new tiny yellow flowers. So

22

that the yellow flower's death is not in vain.

What about the purple flower? You see that because of its down wind position it has been pollinated by the yellow flower's pollen. A little more time passes and another one of nature's cycles unfolds.

The lone purple flower is now showing its first signs of fatigue. You watch it. You don't want to forget a single moment of its wonderful life. Finally, it's time for the lovely purple flower to go to sleep, and it does.

So you look around almost frantically to see if, just like the yellow flowers before, new purple flowers are being born. You scurry around and all you see is the mass of yellow flowers. You know that the yellow flower has flourished, but what about the purple? Did the purple flower pass on its experiences to another generation?

Wait! That, over there. You run up to see if what your eyes see is correct. You see something that looks very much like the purple flower your memory holds dear. The flower is still very young so its petals have not yet opened.

Soon enough, though, it starts to show the first signs of opening up. You look it over again thoroughly to make sure you have the right flower. Yes, there's the strong woody stem with the thorns. The roots must be long and thick, for look how healthy the young plant is. Just a few more moments, wait....and....the flower is now fully opened but this is odd. Everything seems to add up, but not quite. Its petals are still purple, but the colour looks as if it's dulled somewhat. The smell is similar to that of the old purple flower, but not really. Even the texture of the petals are slightly different than before. This is so strange that you take a few steps back and sit down to take all of this in. It's hard to understand why the flower had to go and change when it didn't need to. Not only did the past generations make it strong, but they made it unique too.

Soon, all of the yellow flowers die off and you are left

alone with the hybrid flower. You realise that the yellow flowers don't live as long as the purple flower did, and to top it all off, the hybrid flower is already showing signs of age already. Soon it will die too. There are no other purple or yellow flowers around for it to pollinate. So it is forced to keep its pollen and there will never be a record of the hybrid flower's life. You will wait and see its last dying moment, for it may reinforce the memory of the original purple flower.

The hybrid flower has been dead for a little while now and you are thinking to yourself. Thinking about the beauty and the strengths of the purple flower. Thinking about the yellow flowers which came along and marred the generational pattern of the purple flower leaving only a lonely hybrid. The changes from the purple flower to the hybrid, didn't seem to help or make any difference at all. You are not sure what to think now, because your memory image of the original purple flower is fading but was beautiful the short time it lasted. Sadly, brushing yourself off as you get up, you think to yourself that there must be something else beautiful to look at around here.

"the flower"
was started on
july 7, 1993 at 8:00pm
and completed on
july 8, 1993 at 8:00am
in edmonton

CONTORTION

Contorted
Convict
Control
Loss of
Convalescent
Contact
Con-artist
Artist?
The livelier the message
The more control you lose
The more pain is brought on
The less control you have
Contort
Contorted
Contortion
Distortion
Inside me
Inside you
Inside everyone
So sorry
The calling is late
The position you were put in
The bitterness inside myself
The intimidation I have caused
I have to get
Over all this
Not you
But you do
We all do
Isn't it interesting
How we contort our own

Images of ourselves
To suit our own
Insecurities

IF I LOSE

I'll be listening to the walls
For a heart beat or any other
Sign of life
I don't care if I make
You sad anymore
It's beyond me
Don't cover that X
On your belt
You said anymore
Anymore
And I don't recall
Ever being invited
Or ever being offered
A choice
Anything of mine you have
I never did want
But you can't stay here
Just fall in love
Or fall in line
Fall in love
And fall in line

TURNS ON A DIME

Piss and vultures, broken wings
Dark rituals with no roses
Black viruses eat bacteria
Maggots on a hairless skull
Feeding frenzy slit open
With emptiness bleeding out
On dust and ashes of the past

Crushed angels with ripped chests
Burnt feet and no speech
Out of tune by a broken neck
Lay sadly on cracked windows
With all of their burns displayed
The pointlessness of it all
Is programmed in the brain

The dark idea's always retained
The dark idea's always accepted
So depression is made very real

DISTANCE

There is no one
Who can make my day
When there's
Misappropriation
Of funds
Of feelings
Of movements
Blue smoke
On my horizon
So stay in
Or get out
Get the fuck out
No protection for me
No protection for you
No rush here
Make your own pleasure
On that train ride
Down town
One shot at you
And your remote control
And you're remote control
And you're remote
And you are remote

UNSIGNED

I already know I'm wrong
When I hear her voice
Following me up and down
Through and around
The hills and valleys
Of my little vacation
I am unsigned
What do you know
You know not
You know nothing
You don't know
I am unsigned
I am unsigned
Don't flatter yourself
You didn't discover me
I discovered myself
It is my responsibility
To discover myself
Not yours
Her voice didn't discover me
It followed me
Like a virus that stays in your body
And tires you out
Never leaving your side
The virus was like my shadow
Never leaving my side
Stealing half of my face and half of my show
Wanting part of me
Left in the dark
For people to just notice
But not to take fully in

My shadow is like her voice
Which is like a virus
This is repetitive
This is repetitive
I need something to
Build up my system
I am unsigned
I don't need your signature
To make mine valuable
To make mine worth something
To make mine strong
To make me strong
It takes me awhile
To write all of this down
To make some sense of it
Because it really bothers me
When I really like something
But I'm not really good at it
So I start getting frustrated
And I start thinking of
Sneaking out into the sleeping world
But I won't be approaching you
With a voice like that
Because it has no effect or bearing
On whether I've discovered
Myself or not
Thinking about this
I realise that
I don't want to be here
And I start dreaming
While I drive my car
I look at the scrapes and scars
In and on the cement
Sidewalks and barriers
Thinking that

When your car strikes that barrier
It sends a trail of sparks
And tiny pebbles of cement and steel
Spewing into the air
A long time after you went away
Those scars and divets
With their tiny pieces of steel
In them begin to rust
With all of the regular weathering processes
Leaving large stains of reddish orange
All over the once
Clean and white man made stone
While thinking on that trail
I drifted all the way
To a post office
That smelled of age
And its once white man made walls
Are now stained too
Stained to a sort of dirty beige
That swallows up
The billowy tumbleweed-like plants
That adorn the shelves below the wall stains
Making them look like
A darker stain of beige
On the walls or
Like varicose veins
On the legs of a twenty year old female
They are there
But not really
I sign my soul away
For my packages
At the location
That I stand
Realising that
I dreamt my way here

Why is this so repetitive
Why do I keep bringing up
All these similes, metaphors, symbols
And other worn out factions
Of a language of mine
That's just another worn out faction
Of mine
I'm strong
I'm unsigned
I'm strong
I'm unsigned
Your signature
Reminds me of the stains
That I just dreamt
I'm strong
I'm unsigned
I am strong
I am unsigned

MY EYE

I'm so damn tired
What do I do here
You aren't the object
Of my eye
Load it in
Load it all up
What am I doing here
Load it in
Load it all up
The heat from my dinner
Is fogging up
All of the windows in here
And I don't care
If you're a grandmother
You're no grandmother of mine
How long does it take you
To look that young
About as long as it
Takes me to look that old
About as long as it
Takes you to show
No interest in me
What's it look like outside
What's it look like inside
Even though there is
No sound coming from the radio
I still can't get to sleep
With it on
I'm going on purpose
I am going on a purpose
Stoop to conquer

Stoop to conquer
You never know the words
You spoke or speak
You never could
Understand your words either
And I never could
Or can understand
Why people think
I am older than I am
But I'm so tired now
It's alright
As long as
You aren't the object
In my eye

OBSCURE TO YOU

This is the
Dawning of madness
If you're so bored
Then why go through
With it
I was caring
Just to feel bad
And thanks to that stuff
You fed me before
Everything has the
Same taste of it now
I'm getting off of that chain
And getting on the
Right set of tracks
As soon as possible
Flight to cover is like
Some sort of
Innate releasing
Mechanism
Something pushes me
To move
And I don't know why
It's like I'm
Not supposed
To question it either
This is all related
This is all related
Because pure is
Unrealistic and disgusting
Pure is nonexistent
You get the fuck

Out of here
You know not
What you are doing
For if you did
You wouldn't have
Done it in the first place
For if you did
You would have known
What it would have started
This is all the
Dawning of madness
You know not
What you are doing

HEATING FOR NEPTUNE

I don't want to use my ears anymore
The information of sound
The sound of information
Is hurting my head
Can you hear the earth move
I can
You don't know how I feel
You just say that
Because you'd like to think
You have something
In common with me
That's why all this information
Scrubs (in) my ears too hard
When people say something
Just to convince themselves
And no one else

FEEDERS

I'm being
Force fed
Crap
While I
Vibrate and
Bounce to
Be free
Your crap
Is hollow
Not filling
You say it's
The truth
If so
Why do I
Not believe
You
It is because
You
Have tied
Me up to
Tell me your
Truth

COLOURS

Your brights
Are the same
As her blacks
Both mean
Snot to me
Step on my
Heels
I'll step on your
Head
Who are snot
Think I'm
Lower because
I'm grubby
I'm grubby
On outside
Not inside
You're the
Opposite
Your colours
Won't hide
That snot

BETTER THAN HIS EQUAL

I walked in the room
My throat tightened up
My stomach lurched
And my chest caved in
He is nothing
And insists on making
Me into nothing
That suggests he is my
Equal
NO
I am better than him
I am better than almost
Everyone
Everyone else is my equal
He is not my equal
Never say that
Never imply that
For it's not true
I am tired of hurting myself
I am better than almost
Everyone
No one is better than me
This is not ego
It is truth
Truth that says
I will have to love myself
To exist
I am better than almost
Everyone
Everyone else is my equal
No one is better than me

That is why I reacted
The way I did
Because he hurt me much
And made me think
That he is better than me
That scares me
The fact that I let
Him do this to me
Not to worry
I will show him
How much better I am
By ignoring his stabs
And walking away

I DIE YOU LIE

Wearing thin
My innocence
And virginity out the window
Replaced with
Anger and sadness

Bitterness and madness

Oh yeah
That's how it goes
When push comes to shove
From above your nose

Pull it in your sights
Then push it out
Of your language
The biggest fear
Is I'll fight back

While you chew my back

Oh yeah
Cut me off at the knees
Because that's the only
Way that he sees
I'll burn you in out fame fuck your religion in your ear and eye and mouth and out your rectum mouth full of bricks and cement no ocean's worth that crap no blue no skin you feel something I feel nothing I am nothing you are smaller no love song here so long fuck head face fan in gear two I'M OUTTA HERE!!!

BLACK

Hands down
Tits up
I don't want to be any part
Of generation x
And I am not a slacker
You want to waste
Your time like that
Fine
I am not going to be any part
Of your lazy foolishness
You embarrass me
Waiting waiting
I hope I get turned on
I hope I get turned on
I
Hope
I
Get
Turned
On
You masturbate out of boredom
Your independence is becoming a pain in the ass
It will be a happy song
But it doesn't matter
Because you've been sleeping all along
Turn on the television
And go back to sleep
You don't know where you're going
Because you don't know
Where you came from or
Where you are or

Who you are
Because if you knew the answer
To all of these queries
Then you'd make a change
For the better
But it doesn't matter
You self righteous clown
Reality bites
Only if you can't accept it
But don't worry
If you go back to sleep
It will all pass you by
And you won't notice
Anything at all
But that's all part
Of the ugly beauty of you
And your trend
You don't worry or notice
Anything at all
All hands down
All tits up
All heads down
Maybe you do notice
But you're too tired
To make a difference
Mister slacker
I think that the
Only reason I write this
Is to try and
Jump start you out of your apathy

NOT EGO

Sign your name here
Because once in awhile
You get away
Walls are a necessity
In a modern society
You just want it clean
I guess it's alright
I'm not ready to see you yet
And I need some distance
And I have a feeling that
I'll never see any ink from you
On any paper from me
And I'll have to be satisfied
With my ink
On my paper
I guess it's alright
It's alright
Because people who walk into my life
For brief glimpses of my time
Can call me god
But people who see me talk my write
And come to me with open eyes
Can call me friend
Or better yet
Lover
Hey you
Yes you
You who forgot to sign your check
Before you mailed it
Do you get this?
Do you get it?

Or do you just think it's beneath you
Well
It's not
It's above you
But to all my friends and lovers
It's on the exact same level as they are
That's why they
Come to me
With open eyes
And I never have
And never will
Turn them away
Do you want to know
What the funny thing about you is
It's that I won't ever have to turn you away
You did that job for me

PROVOKING DRAMA

Fear
Gives me strength
It's a slow risk
This is the time
This is the place
I'm going to leave you
Without a trace
I don't stroll anywhere
I walk every where
Why is it that
When I am alone
I am antisocial
And when you are alone
You are an artist
Muscles and church
Muscles and church
What does fear do to you?
Crop tight baby
Crop tight
And as you were
And as you was
And as you will always be
What does fear do to you?
I'm not happy to miss you
You're not in my house
And I'm proud to say
That I'm not in yours

NASCENT

The ring on your finger
Is far too tight
And I'm not the one
Who jumped the median
You did
Not me
You did
I can't tell if
It's thunder or
Just someone
Running around upstairs
Maybe it would help
If I filed down
All of the rough edges
One is one too many
One too many
One to many
One all the way to many
All caught in a morass
After I was ossified
By a canon
All your fault
All your fault
Now you say that
I must seek retribution
All of these hands waving
All of these legs waving
In some sort of feeble parade
No, actually there are
No hands here
Just paws

Dirty filthy paws
Would it bring you down
Will it bring you down
If I talk this way
About all this show
At a concert
Is just like the
Ring on your finger
Cutting off the circulation
And with a loud
Clap off thunder
You hurtle yourself
Over the top of the median
And into the waiting
Mass of paws, heads and legs
What a parade
What a show
It's better than
The movies
In all of the
Fuss and rhetoric
I forget about
The retribution
I was seeking
And I finally
Forgot about the canon
Your canon
And the morass
My morass
We were a one
We were a monolith
Being told what we saw
And what to read
The rough edges
Will remain

The rough edges
Will remain
And then when
It's all done
The security guards
Will move on
To another window
To dress
To address
And when the roadies
Have finished
Their cleaning
I'll go home
To coddle my bruises
And what of you
How does that ring
On your finger feel now
Is it a little more tight
Than it was before
You walked up onto that stage
The river used to run
In front of us both
A free flowing river
Then you walked up
Onto that stage
Onto your stage
And the river that
Ran in front of me
Abruptly ended

BEHIND MY BACK

A poet is a thief
I am not a thief
They make you wonder why
You make you wonder why
I make you wonder why
Pulling hope out of your skull
I am a god
I made you up eat rotten meat
I step on you
When I walk
Wonder why
Because that's how we all
Work
I'll sit with all the garbage
And let you walk
In goodness and get fat
At that time I'll be
Waiting and ready
No one will call me
A brother
If god is within us
We assassinate him
Every day
I've noticed that
Something good never happens
I always turn around
And see a thief or what I made

YOU BASTARD

As I write this
My hand shakes
My stomach is rebelling
My spelling is off
And I feel sick
Yes I am disturbed
Yes I am sick
No one will ever
Hear my words
Ever again
My stomach
Turns inside out
No one will ever
Hear my words
Ever again
You made me do something
I have never done
You made me into
Something I hate
Even more than myself
My offensive
Is offensive
I am sorry
No one will
See or hear me again
I am sorry
I hate you
For making me
Kill myself again

HAPPY FUCK YOU FACE

You shouldn't have given me the chance
Cos there's no reason in my death
And now I'll tear you apart
From limb to limb with flowers

Take your happy fuck you face
And place it far underground
I don't feel like looking at you
Anymore than I do a butterfly

Now to get to my point in this:
Don't try and ruin me with
Your happy fuck you face
Cos I'll turn you into dried flowers

I WOULD LIKE TO KILL THE PRESIDENT

Cats still fight
Over a dead nightingale
Calling me a beast
While eating their candy
How much does your
Show cost me
On the outside
Show cost them
On the inside
Under and below you
Show cost you
Show cast you
Die cast you
It's no wonder
I hate you
It's no wonder
They hate you
You call them
Less than me
Ironic that you
Only call them
When you need them
Fuck your claims
You've eaten the
Bird and the cake
Leaving none for them
And a foul taste
Is left in my mouth
That's why
I will kill
The president of the United States

HAWK

Perched on a rock
By a church
Exhaust filling my nostrils
Like the old ladies
Perfume over top
Sun's bright
I've come to wake you
You who keeps me
At arms length
I'm watching and
Waiting to strike
And be rude
It's like the
Various odours
Are fuelling me
But I know
The truth
The truth is
My anger and
Frustration fuels me
Helps me ignore
The gaping hole
Wound in my chest
I'm perched and
Waiting to scream
On to you
For whatever it takes
Bye bye meat
Hello sunshine
And emptiness

RUST IN YOUR LUNGS

Rust
The bending of my mind
Rust
The bending of your will
Rust
My bleeding hands
Rust
Your bleeding hearts
Rust

So call it
Don't stop it
Cos I'll push you
Push you down

I want your lungs
So I can see everything
I want your lungs
So I can foul you

So call it
Don't stop it
Cos I'll push you
Push you down

I want your lungs
So I can break you
I want your lungs
So I can brain you

So call it
Don't stop it
Cos I'll push you
Push you down

I want your lungs
So I can fuck you
I want your lungs
So I can annoy you

So call it
Don't stop it
Cos I'll push you
Push you down

Rust
The breaking of my mind
Rust
The breaking of your soul
Rust
The breaking of my hands
Rust
The breaking of your trust
Rust
Rust

PUSHING

You don't have
Much farther
To go
I'll tell you
Right now

I want your lungs

Not your heart
Or your brain
Your lungs
I'll tell you
Right now

You don't push

You don't have
Much farther
To go
Before I push
You back

I'll pull your lungs

Out
And watch you
Twitch in confusion
Scratch at you chest
Push at your head

Push at mine

And I'll steal your lungs

BAD TIMING

Don't lose your napkins
And put out your pope
Put out your own pope
In all trust
There is a risk of betrayal
What's it worth to you?
Put out that
God damned addiction
Bring on the tar
That covers your
Face and costume feathers
You've run out of luck
Pick up the tempo a bit
And you'll walk away
With your sight intact
Intact in taste
Tastefully tactful
Isn't in your
Dictionary or thesaurus
I'm very restless
Sunny and hot all day
Rainy and wet all night
It's all published by revenge
Thinking about the
Beautiful one and how
I will lay with her
Waiting those nights out
Trying to sleep
Properly again
Talking to her and
Hearing her say that

Now is not the time
Over and over it will play
Over and over in my head
Just as loud as the
Thunder crashing outside
Outside of my head
And I think a little harder
About how easy
It would be to
Turn to alcohol as my mate
No
I won't listen to this again
No
I won't listen to this anymore
I look outside my cage
And feel the cool air
From outside flow
Over my bare chest
It's the same cool air
I feel when I
Dream of laying with her
The beautiful one
Who told me that
Now is not the time
Or was it
Now is not the right time
Or
Now is not a good time
I can't remember
There's no way out
I'm trapped here
By my own guilt
And the way I rush
Into something headlong
Or is it head short

Or is it head first
Or head last
Yes
I shared some of this with you
But I still feel
It's nothing that special
Then if that's true
Then why do I clutch it
Tight against my chest
And I could tell you
But then I'd have to kill you
I really do know
Honestly
Honestly
I don't know what's going on
What if I came knocking
On your door
Would you let me in
With good will
To lay me on
Knowing full well that
I'll only come in
Times of trouble
Or would you open the door
And snicker as
I fell into your coterie
Would you just
Wipe your face off
And wash your hands of it
Even if you lost your napkins
My mind feels as if
It's gone through a war
And my body feels
Like it's about to go into one
You look much older

In the daylight
And I feel much younger
Sitting here with you
And I feel much younger
Than you
The beautiful one
In my addiction
My addictive thoughts
And my timing is off
Way off lost
Lost in a cornfield
With no buildings in sight
With the bright sun
Pummelling down on my head
And my thoughts
And any other part
That's exposed
With heat so strong
It holds the wind
And all other forms of life down
That's where I stand
In the middle of
All my wants and needs
For myself
Being sandblasted into
Doubts and uncertainties
By myself
In myself

CONUNDRUM

As the crow flies
Take him down
From the cross
So he can listen to
The tape loop of himself
Take him down
From your cross
Why keep on analysing
The differences
When we could be
Finding similarities
Take them down
From your cross
But not in my backyard
Save you more?
Save you more what?
Where's the one
Who'll draw the line
Move along
In a baby carriage
As the crow flies
What goes around
Comes around
No one to draw a line
Aggravating the situation
Do you want to bind
You have the answer
Do you know
You have the answer
Collectively
You're unconscious

It's all over
Before it even started

WITCH TRIALS

Too much direct
Evidence is always
Aimed at uniqueness
So a movie says
Same old same old
End of the road
And got my goat
With a sonic laugh
This goes farther
Than forever
It's all just a blur
It's always just
A blur of a vision
Which is too direct
Never get no pay
If you're too open
Open is direct
Which is unique
Maybe that explains
Why fingers point
At me constantly
Same old same old
End of the movie
Got my same old?
Too much direct
Evidence is aimed
At uniqueness and
Heroes of the peoples
Heroes just make
The peoples notice
Their pities and mistakes

All the more, all the more
Same old same old
End of the movie
Got my same old?

PASSING THE BUCK

We'll let god know
We will do our best
I nod out loud
Thinking that
We are all a
Crowded generation
Crowded with noise
Crowded with problems
Crowded with people
And more problems
And more people
It's some kind of fire
We haven't learned
To put out
It's all someone else's fault
But we can't
Remember who's
Because it started
So long ago
Well, no I'm not pregnant
With anybody else's ideas
But my own
You're a recurring ailment
Making me hide
I'm through hesitating
I'm going to admit that
I like the smell of history
And I'll let you know
That mine smells
The sweetest to me
I nod out loud

You're way over-rated
And I'm going
To lie down and
Sleep in that cemetery
We are a crowded generation
I'm trying to
Stand in the middle
Of the game of solitaire
And all of the crowds
We are the crowded generation
And I just want some room
I'm so aggravated
With the most definite
Signs of fatigue
In this world of
Alien sightings
We'll let god know
I nod out loud
We'll let god know

EIGHTEEN

I let you get your way
I just gave you a bone
Why don't you just tell me
I sold out
Because I wasn't sure
Who I'd meet
Because I wasn't sure
Who I was going to meet
I know who I wanted to meet
I want to know the person
Who signs my cheques
But I met someone
Who was even better than that
And I loved her the
Moment she shook my hand
I loved how strong her grip was
When our hands shook
And those voices started up
I always hear voices
Shuffling through the back
Of my head
Saying my name is worth money
Or something like that
I wish I could kill those voices
Or something like that
While my body works in
Solemn foolery
While my brain works in
Solemn foolery
While my writing works in
Solemn foolery

I'm in your face?
You're in my face
Eye of the beholder
Eye of the beholder
Who made me into the one
Who's supposed to boost
Everyone else's ego
Except for mine anyways?
I mean that
You can't be different
In a construction crew
I mean that
If you're waiting
For me to say something poetic
You'll have to wait a long time
I have no plans as of yet
To say anything poetic or
To say anything like that
Or something like that
I see you
But you don't see me
Or something like that
There's no way on this planet
I'm going to find a way
To tie this all together
I just give people a bone
Maybe that's why I get
Nothing I ever want
From anybody
The cheques were nice
The grip was special
But it's all gone now
And I'm not sure if
It will ever come back
Or if it will ever be enough

If it did come back
Or something like that

I'm just a half writer
Whose timing is never right
I'm tired of my pen
And tired of my watch
Stopping too soon
I'm sick of feeling
Whatever I do is incomplete

HEAD ON THE TABLE

I don't recommend it
While it's raining
No reflections here
On my chair
I didn't mean to put
The dirt on the
Wrong side
Of my chair
I didn't mean that
It was important
It's just that all
I'm trying to do
Is drink mercury
And try to keep
Alive in this jungle
I don't recommend it
There's got to be
Something I can do
Some way of
Getting out of
This anything
Anything
I got to do to get out of this
Somehow
No hobnobbing
Just my filthy
Reflections and
Dirt and wrong ways
I don't recommend it
I just don't recommend it

Blew inside me
From your outside
Means nothing to you
But everything to me
Outside thorns
Inside me inside
Mine
No flowers here
Just weeds
I could shut you down
But you strike first
Fast and flee
And I'm left down
Just
Thinking about
You and me

SMOKE FLY

Smoke screen
Smoke fly
Smoke screen
Smoke fly
Are you happy
Are you
Mind worn
Muscles torn
Appearance thorns
Make
Break
Or take
Smoke screen
Fake
Smoke fly
Bake
No not
Not on
Me
You are happy
Smoke screen
I'm not
In or
Out
You have
The one
That I don't
But we
Both have
Just a
Smoke fly

Smoke screen

R-33

The pink slip
Self condemnation
Where to live
Fuck you
You should die
Thank you
I will live
The D.E.W. is set off
No labour no play
Because you
Have to pay
To play
Seeking out nothing
Wishing for anything
Sighting something
But none of it
Is really there
Only future issues
I worry about you
I worry about me
I worry about nothing
I'm low
I'm a crack
Walk on me
It's alright
Music's the life
Of my dreams
And my reality
Without work
I'm so much
As a crack

To be laid off
And walked on

KILLING MY SKY

Going through the coal mine
Of my brain
Killing my sky
With my dusty images
Of the past grunge
Killing my sky
By clipping my wings
Hope a wind passes through
Tearing up all the dirt
Giving my hand a hand
Will anything lock the
Freezer that holds all
The extremes so fresh
Lock them all up for good
Lock them up
The years of past are done
The years to come yet
Will be a curse
Will be a hex
If I can't lock the webs up
Webbing of my past
Killing my sky
With coal dust in my mouth
In my eyes
In my ears
In my nose
In my heart
Killing my sky
In my heart

SLEEP ON

I don't believe in anything
You
Myself
Anyone
Anything
I won't fight anymore
My dreams
Are
Killing
Me
We are all guilty of my nothing
My
Inferiority
Non
Miracle
The island is wearing apart
Compromises
Make me
Go nowhere
Nothing is right anymore
Quiet
Time
Is coming
Is wanting
Hit me hard maybe I'll wake

BABY

Do you want my name
I want yours
I need yours
But do you want my name
But do you need my name

Do you want to know me
Who am I
Who I am
Do you wish to know me
Not just my name but me

I want to know you
I want closeness
For time
For more
For me
For you
And for both
And for more

VAGUELY RADIANT

I slept in napalm
Please hang the fucking savages
Because I'm tying myself in knots
The beep in the dark
Terminates the napalm
And a corpse awakens
I am afraid to open
Because I don't think
I could stand it
Because I don't think
Anyone could stand it
I am a dull day

FUTURE'S TWISTED BREAK

Burning an addictive future
The green cannot be enough
Screens and screens of light
Give cold logical explanations

The cure must be in advance
Or the fight for machines is wrong
Colour documents are so small
When everyone is missing senses

Paradise is controlled by buttons
Natural quality is brushed away
Lost and forgotten like paints
Too little time we're all rushed

Every month is a december
Cold and mass produced
Flying so fast into shiny discs
So planned performances are only

I'm at such an utter loss
Caves and branches and dirt
To gears and chips and clocks
What could be the next phase

TAKE THIS OR LEAVE

I'm sad
Sad
Sad
An angry
Sad
Sad
Nobody
Likes a
Loser
No one
Wants me
No one
I want
Wants me
I am
To be
Alone
No one
Wants
A loner
No one
Wants to
Take all
Of this
No one
Wants
All of me
I don't
Come in
Parcels
You have

To take it all
Or leave it all
I am
So
Sorry
A sad
Sad
Sad
Sorry

Odd one in
Beamed
In a cloudy
Forest
Nailed and
Caged in
Look around
And in
And at
Me
And analyse
Don't bother
I'm not
In a zoo
Or a fish bowl
Back off
You're not
Wanted
Around
And in
And at
Me
I won't stand
Or ask
For it
So tour
Away from
My language

HOW COULD YOU HEAR

It costs me so much
To read to you
Do you listen
You do, do you
I wish I knew
Why I do this
Do you know why
You do, do you
I hit myself again

I end up going to
My compartment
Wanting to be held
By anybody
But instead I hear
Someone else's problem
Thundering through
My walls of halls
And think what right
Do I have to
Hold sorrow

I look around and
See anybody is not
Here to hear me or
To hold me
I can't hold myself
My finger tips are too cold
I can't touch myself
It makes me sick
I make me sick

Let my razors
Touch me
I let my blood
Hear me

I'd like to cut my chest
Wide open and give you
What's inside me
But I'm sure
Sure as eggs
That's what inside of me
Is of no use to you

I feel like swallowing
My razor blades whole
After all of this
Are you still my friend
You are, are you
It costs me so much
To write to you
To read to you
To scream to you
Do you hear me
You do, do you

WINTER ON THE BUS

They say this is the dead season
Now I understand why on the bus
All the drab and dreary colours
That match the sadness in the faces

The earth colours, the dull colours
The moss greens, the wood browns
The sand beiges, the ash greys
The navy blues and the midnight blacks

The people's faces and their talk
The tired expressions and pointless mumbling
The stares out the window
And the young ones who look different

The young ones like me getting older
Who feel on the verge of tears
Who genuinely feel tired
Who feel like dying but you can't

You can't fully die though
Because there's work to do
Only part of you will die
Because it's the dead season

The cold season the hibernation season
The season you try to keep warm
But can't on the bus, in the line
Because your dying slowly in work

And this is the season you notice it the most

I feel like
Cutting my chest open
I feel like
Slitting my own throat
And letting my guilt
Bleed out of me
My shame
Bleed out of me
My regret
Bleed all out of me
Leaving my skin in a puddle
And my bones in a pile

QUIET

Are you listening to me
Don't you listen to me
Have you ever listened to me

I'm crying
I am not with me
This is not my seam
I am not among you
I am burning
Screaming
Crying

I am crying
I'm inside out
My heart is collapsed
I am talking to you
But you are blind
To my
Crying

Deaf to my
Screaming
Dull throbbing in my chest
Around my skull
But you are deaf to me
Your screen is up so
You are deaf to my sights

Are you listening to me
Don't you listen to me
Have you ever listened to me

Are you listening to me

HAVE AN APPLE

Have an apple
It keeps the
Doctor away
No block shifts
Hope toward
A second accident
Compliments or
Complaints
I shall make my
My way home
I hate you
I'm gone
The only way
The only way
I'm gone
The closest I'll
Ever get to you
Is sitting in a bus
And watching your
Vehicle drive by
We could touch
But our machines
Get so in the way
People are ignoring us
Keep the doctor away
Because people are
Just ignoring us
My ball is in my
Gap in my stomach
I wish both would
Leave me

Leave me with
Sleep that corrodes
My brain like
Rust on a weathered
Aging ships' deck
Using different
Coloured pens to
Sustain my superstition
Or buying lotto tickets
To keep my
Hopes up or
To keep my
Apple ripe all
The while ignoring
The people ignoring
And shifts and
Accidents and
Compliments and
The smell of
The rotting apple
That's no good
For baking or
Keeping the doctor
Away
Just bringing
The smell of the
Fears of the
Future bringing
Brings to me

FOREST (LOST IN A)

I never wanted to say goodbye
What were you
Inside of me
On an angle to me
I should have taken my pill
I need a crowd
So I know not to take advantage of you
I need some sleep
I need to be bored
I need to be relaxed
I'm lying here hearing myself changing
Not liking it one bit
Burning like a ball
Of newspaper in a fire pit
Looking at the person next to me
And my eyes are changing at her
And my eyes are changing too fast
Because I'm not like anything
Anymore than before
I start to think I should
Probably just die and
Instead I go look for
Change for the bus
I try to live for today but
I'm too busy thinking of tomorrow
A forest of bluish white mould
In a dark wet cavern
Somewhere where buses can't go
And somewhere where I won't get inside of me
And somewhere where I know what you were
And what I wasn't

I should have taken my pill
Good bye

WINE

I don't want
My fortune told
Told to me
I don't need
My fortune told
Told to me
I don't need
My future told
Told to me
I'll find out
What it is
When it's time
Speaks to me
Am I just falling
Between the cracks
Am I first
Or am I last
Burning on
Am I going
Down a
One way street
Am I going
Down a wrong way
Street
The right way
Or am I going
Down a right way
Street
The wrong way
I feel as if
None of them

Are mine
None of which
Are mine
My futures
Are told
None of which
Are mine
Sometimes our
Senses fail us
A beautiful woman
Sitting across from me
Sitting up
With her eyes shut
Is she looking
At her future
Her past
Am I making this
Into more than it is
She's a tired beautiful woman
In a nurses' uniform
It's almost midnight
She is tired
And going home to bed
Tired of wearing
The shoes
The light blue uniform
The slip
Her hair tied that way
And all
Is she
Is she seeing something
Let it ferment
I'm not singing
The same refrain
Over and over

Anymore
Seeing her
Turning towards myself
And looking away
Quickly like
She's seen something
That scares her
I don't know
What more I can say
About all of this
I'll let it all ferment
I don't want my future
Told to me
I'll find my way
Around all these
Dead end streets
Eventually
None of them
Are mine
None of which
Are mine
None of these
Are mine
I lost that woman
Just before midnight
When I get tired and sad
The most
Nurse nurse
Get me a doctor
Not a fortune teller
A doctor
I need help
With my present
Not my future

MOTHER TO BE

I felt like she was asking
Me to be a father
Of a child who was only her's
And not mine
The real father departed
And her last lover loves her no more
She looked very desperate
And everyone else
Has their hats on backwards
The days getting longer
The nights getting shorter
The days getting shorter
The nights getting longer
What does it matter
If you can't see straight
Maybe I read too much
Into situations that
Mean something to me
I could never be either to her
And she probably knows this
She just needs something
That is firm
So she can hold onto it
I dissect things too much
I look at all the new colours
Springing to life in front of my eyes
I look at her with her uncertainty
And she's trying to let life grow inside of her
And everyone around her
Is wearing their hats on backwards
How can you see straight

When only a select few can
We're not sure of anything anymore
I'm not comparing myself to herself
It's just I wish I could
Do more for her
Than I already do
Which is just sit here and write
And talk to her trying to
Help her understand
Something I don't understand
Something that is too big
For me to understand
I felt like she was asking me
And I felt like giving her an answer
But I'll never know the right answer for her

The sun is smiling down on me and I want to return the favour. But for some reason I can't. Even when I try, I can't. Or won't. It seems I am good at making myself depressed but not happy. Happy. I should be. But I'm not. Days like this are strange. I feel like lying in the sun forever. But you can't because it gets dark eventually. At least you know that the dark will go on regularly as long as the sun lives. It's just that one of the things I hate the most is. It is. It's this. My darks seem to last much longer than the lights. Much longer than what I want. This bothers me so much. I want a cure. And that's this. And that's that.

BODY OVER MIND

Sometimes when my friends
Go away
I forget them
Out of sight
Out of mind
Out of mind
Out of sight
And the roof is rotting
Over there
And I don't know why
And everyday at the same time
I see the same person in a window
Over there
Across from the same window
I now look through
And I wonder if he notices me
Noticing him
Noticing me
Noticing him
I am my worst enemy today
And I don't know why
And I wonder if he notices me
In this state
You know I know
It's like that woman
Who feeds two lines
Of unemployed homeless people
One on her right
And one on her left
Both at the same time
People who are looking for a catharsis

Or some sort of truss
The roof is rotting
The roof is rotting
The roof is rotting
Give me something
Food, some sort of catharsis
Truss, trusses anything
Looking at and noticing that man
Makes me hungry and weak
He's the same person
I see everyday
And so am I
I need to change my
Seating arrangements
I don't want anything
From you anymore
But I know that's
An attitude I dream of having
Like friends who should
Be forgotten who I can't forget
Like that damn roof rotting over there
Food, catharsis, truss
Food, catharsis, truss
Anything
Anything
Why am I sitting here anyways?

THE DRAGON (GORGE)

Walking in the hallway
I can tell when you
Look away on purpose
Can't you find a
Better way to deal with it
Sitting in the hallway
Listening to the constant rumbling
Of all the vehicles outside
Wondering what's driving
Wondering who's driving
All this scares me to sleep at night
Because I never really see
Just who drives all of that noise
Just what makes all of that noise
It all scares me to sleep
It all scares me to write
It all forces me to write
Madness in greatness
Must not go unwatched
The place inside your bosom
Where you keep hidden
Your innermost secrets
And the pit in the
Bottom of my stomach
Where I hold mine
Are both equal
They are both empty
Moiety
They are moiety
Both
Empty both moiety

Empty wanton figures of grief
And sometimes when
(On the rare occasion)
I'm feeling strong and invulnerable
I think that I would
Be able to deal with it
The both being empty
Because of a gorge
Of human flaws
That are too big
That are too small
The gorge is too small
The gorge is too big
Whichever
I'd be able to deal with it
With your flaws
With no problems at all
Everybody has flaws
Can't you find a
Better way of dealing with it
Everybody has the same
Human flaws

Hello,
Good morning
It's so nice to see you
I also see that
As usual you are a little late
As usual
I'll be writing around the corner
And I'll meet you
Under the walkway
And I will meet you
Under the walkway
And I see your head turn

That protection on purpose
I don't want to see you that way
And whichever you choose
Won't be anywhere near
The best protection under the sun
Under the sun
Madness
Under you
Under the walkway
Under the sun
Watch it
Watch now
Watch it all now
Watch all great ones?
Why don't you watch me?
You were the one
Who called me a great one
I never called myself that
Watch all great ones
I see now
And try to reason it all out
But can't you see that
You'll never see my will
My strong will
But I don't in a bad way
It's a good way
The way I mean it
And then we will
See who has the best protection
We will see
Because right becomes wrong
And wrong a right
Around here
Around here
All the strangers

Do you know that?
Do you
Do you know that
If you're going to do a lie
You'd better be prepared to die
Or else
Hold yourself and watch it

Hold yourself for a little while
And you try to reason it all out
Your beauty won't fill my pit
And my tongue won't repair anything
That it hasn't broken
It can't
Have you your choice yet?
Do you
I see that my question
Was answered with
The toss of your head
None are great ones
Don't you know that
Do you know it
I'm sitting in the hallway
The unsung hallway
Wishing all the noise
That's scaring me one the outside
Wouldn't keep on driving me to sleep
And that empty feeling
With that god damned gorge
Would just fuck off and die
So it would make my jaunt
To the walkway a little easier
What a morning
Flaws and all
I'm still avoided by your eyes

It's that protection on purpose
Protection from strangers
Bearing facts
Like none are great ones
Do you know it?
But do you believe it
None are great ones
Right is a wrong
Wrong is a right
None are great ones
Some are madness
Do you know it
Do you
Believe it
Admit it
Know it
I've done nothing wrong
So I can't repair anything
I see that by your walk in the hallway
Your choice is made but
Will you ever understand that choice you made
Do you understand it
Watch it
Believe it
Admit it
Know it
Do you

THE OTHER NOTE

Blocks and ashes, wishes and fear
Plastic sky burning action smoke
Swelter dry blue caress the stamp

Give me credit no taste and care

Termites in glass beige, harmonics
Rapid imploding, don't you get it?
Flip none grasses and greens energy
Alcoholic infested boxes of crates

You don't care of the masks

Benched salted candy and dope
I'm falling into canned darkness

Bright fabric won't help any

FACE DUST

What did I do wrong
I can barely contain myself
What did I do wrong
I didn't even look
At your face
There's thunder all around
Sounds the same
As oncoming sirens to me
I wish I could
Sit in a corner of a room
And curl up in a ball
And watch and listen
To Ry Cooder play
All his landscapes out
But everyone speaks of
Ry Cooder this way
It's nothing new
I don't want an
Art show just yet
Maybe later
And you with bracelets
From your wrist
To your shoulder
I wrecked my father's' car
Without his permission
I had to leave the room
With the incense and words
I walked outside
I don't mind
The cold or rain
In fact I stood under

A drain briefly
Water pouring out
Onto my hat
Onto my head
Watching the water
Run and drip and drop
Off of the edge
Of the brim of my hat
In front of my eyes
I go back into
The warmth of
My place of stay
And instead of
Embracing the warmth
I wait to be slapped
Looking down at the floor
Holding my head down
Holding my hands together
Like a little child that
Hasn't got the same
As everyone else
And he feels it isn't fair
And he wants to say something
But is too scared to speak up
And I should be writing
Much smaller now
And I wish I could
Hold that body
That I briefly held
Again
And again the thought
Is just black and white sound
Or maybe I was
Just cadging a ride
The move was made

And this is
Just more paper and ink
And I am
Just another one
Who forgot to
Hold onto something
When he had it

CATHEXIS

Maybe if you were normal
I could love you
But it's pretty big crowd
With smoke and alcohol
For people to swim in
It matches the humidity
Maybe if you were normal
Somebody would recognise me
Maybe if I was normal
Somebody somewhere in this
Writhing seething mass of prostitution
Someone would recognise
Something other than
The drunks trying to
Make sense of each other
Abreact
Abreaction to the mass of noise
That's building and spiralling
From the front almost as if
It's going to sweep us all away
Into the garbage dumpster out back
If that is what you call your god
From what I have just seen
He is no god of mine

CRUSHED AND TAUGHT

Grey hills mounted on bricks
Snow and glue melt and
Keep me from coming or going
I know nothing till it falls on me

Crushing and teaching me

Wind and papers fly past me
While I sit on the orange and metal
My feet are sore, I'm not sure why

They haven't been broken or taught though

I'm an egg! No, no eggs here
Just tar and mud so I can't move
I'm still stuck in this boring mess
Ten days is not that long, but

These clocks can't crush and teach me

Give me a chance, I'll show you
I won't lose anything (not even imagery)
Centralised pain and scum
No! I have a brain I can work

But if you won't crush me, I can't be taught

PROSCENIUM

I was lying beside you
But it felt like
All of our talking
Was being done
Over the phone
I am Mr. White
Believing in something
That's not true
And having to do
Something about it
The gods are crazy
And don't you
Forget it
First things last
No smoke here
Here, in this room
I think it was
Never really
Interdependent
Most of us have
Been inbred into
Somebody who
Will conform
You feel you have
Been exposed
Trying to be
Accepted by the group
And not accepted
By the one
By a one
All of this

Laying beside you
And talking
Over a phone

PRANK CALL

Imagine
Someone calling you up
And saying
That they know for a fact
That you don't exist
And then hanging up
And that same someone
Doing that everyday
Doing that for everyday
For years and years
Imagine
Imagine
That someone
All of a sudden
Stops calling
And never calls you again
And now you start to think
Think as the days go past
And no phone call
You start to expect
That ring and voice again
Everything is so quiet now
At least when
The calls came
You could convince yourself
That you do exist
After that voice leaves
You in your silence
Now you think that
Maybe the calls have stopped
Because now you

Don't really exist so
Why bother making a call
When no one exists anymore
You can't call someone
Who doesn't exist
Where's that damn call
Where's that damn call
I do exist, I do
And you just call me
Just once more
And I'll prove it to you
I will
But no more calls come
No more
Do you really exist
You're not sure anymore
Because you can't
Prove it to anyone, even yourself
You can't even prove it to
The one who made the calls before
Now
Start all over again
Start it all over again in your head
Imagine
Someone calling up
And saying
That they know for a fact
That you don't exist
And then hanging up
Imagine
Imagine
All the doubt coming back
All the time falling back
Imagine
Imagine that

DRY NEST (HAYKU)

Four people are travelling in a jeep to a city a little ways away. It's a four lane highway with a large grass median in between. Two lanes on one side. Two lanes on the other.

They are travelling south.

They all know where they are going presently. After that...Who knows?

Not them.

There are two females and two males. The weather is bright, hot and sunny. It's a beautiful day.

Suddenly, without warning, the female who is driving STOPS. There are two steers in the middle of the road. Their heads are together as if they are trying to force each other out of each other's way.

The two females in the front are confused

One of the two males in the back is bored.

The other male is sad.

It looks like a photograph, one that the sad male has seen before because the photograph is world famous. If the three others have seen the photograph they are not letting on. And we are not about to find out because now the bored male and the confused females are agitated and want to keep moving. So they drive around the aggressive cows, not bothering to ask the sad male in the back if he wants to move on, and speed away. Leaving behind the immobile steers and part of the sad male. Leaving all that behind with the sad male starring out the back window. Tension rises in the vehicle and the sad male has a good idea why. It's because he is not supposed to look back. He's not supposed to look back. He's doing something that he was not supposed to do.

That was the last time

that he ever did something

that he was not supposed to do.

To him the weather felt stormy. Even though it was still beautiful outside of their time capsule. He thought that his eyes would start to run. So to stop it all he began to write.

And again,
that was the last time
that he ever did something
that he was not supposed to do.

I went out walking this morning
And this woman
Got angry with me
Because when she asked me
To call her a cab I answered no
Later I thought about
Bands who tell me
To play their music loud
On their albums
I only play someone else's' music
The way I want to
Not the way they want it to be played
I'll play it the way I want to
I'll play it the way I want to
You should do the same
You should do the same
But there are many factors
And you take it down
And you take it down anyways
Don't take it down
Just because they cut it down
Leave it up
So it can go higher
What is the concept?
Let it go to the top of the spiral

But there are many factors
That make someone
Rise up and take a big bite
Out of the salt lick
While I read slowly
By everyone's standards
I read slowly
I read slowly
To make sure I don't miss anything
It was a failed surgery
It was a failed attempt to make me right
From something
That everyone thought was wrong
Make the incision
Make the incision
Cut me open and try to make me bleed
In the right way
In the way that they thought was right
I don't know what I'm saying
I don't know what they did
Is that why I don't know what I'm saying
You took it away
You took it all away
Whenever I feel this
Whenever I feel like this
You took it away
Whenever I feel like this
I feel like eating those
Damn green candy mint leaves and
Picking up the nearest camera
And making it and myself
Do our thing
You took it away
And all I can remember
Is that when I started

Thinking about all of this
The weather at the time
Wasn't all that bad
And watching for the
Red light to turn green
I was distracted by
Two people in the van
In front of me
Kissing and not paying attention
To the red light gone green
And when I started rethinking
All of this
It was almost a bloody blizzard
And I was distracted
By the fact that
I like winter
Because it makes me feel strong
And now it's all slipping away
Because
You took it away

The sad one looks up and notices that the male next to him is still bored and that the females in the front are more beautiful than ever.

He doesn't know where he is going.

He wants to make the others stop what he thinks they are doing. He wants to write. He wants to read a book. He wants to write a book and have them read it.

He starts squirming deeper in his seat. The three others in the car start smiling.

Everything is all right.

It's all going right the way it's supposed to be going.

He starts to cry and thinks that in one minute he will start peeling the skin on his face off. Before this, he notices that one of the perfect, lovely females is watching him. It's the one that he wishes he could just slip his hand across her cheek just once. She is smiling at him as he starts to twist and implode inside. He is now scratching all of the flesh on his face off. He bleeds all over himself and his seat. He doesn't notice that the beautiful female is still watching him with the same smile on her face.

It is a smile of wonder. She wonders when he will figure out that he has to keep on his path of complexities. Doing things he's not supposed to do so others can keep on their path of simplicities, doing things they are supposed to do. She wonders when he will figure out that if he wasn't around, then there would be no one around questioning where they were going.

Her soft white skin on her perfectly rounded bones with that silk like blonde hair framing it all. She continues to smile. Making her blue eyes more blue and her white teeth more white.

She turns around to let him cry on his own.

started this piece on
october 3rd, 1993
finished this piece on
november 6th, 1993
in edmonton

EXIT IS A SAFE PLACE

LAB 1

Remorse.

Remorse is what I feel. When I see the scars on my body. When I feel the scars on my body. They aren't scars. They are canyons. Bigger and deeper than the grand canyon could ever dream to be. And you all know how big that is. And you all know that the grand canyon is bigger and deeper than you all. You all know this. Even I, but there are always exceptions to the rules. There is always an exception to every rule. Understand? By the end maybe you will. Maybe you'll see why all the repetition is needed when I speak. When I scream. Maybe in the end you'll see what I've taken away from everyone. Maybe in the end you'll see what everyone has taken from me. Maybe in the end you'll see what I've taken from me. From myself. From I. From I unto you I will let you touch me and my canyons. And maybe in the end you'll understand all of the repetition and all of my guilt and all of my remorse. Maybe, too many maybes for right now. On and on with my tell and show. Maybe maybe maybe. If if if. Join me. Join me? Join me. Join me at the walls of my city and see all of the ruins inside. See how we all pick a poison and choose a tribe and play along. My game just got out of hand.

If (another if) I tell you this maybe (another maybe) I'll understand my guilt and learn to live with it a little better. Maybe (another maybe) when you hear me write all of this down, if (another if) you want to, you'll understand your guilt. Understand all of those sharp pangs of myopic guilt and live (leave with this?) with this a little better.

I speak in another language and it bothers me just as much as it bothers you (maybe (another maybe!!)) but I hope we both can bear with it until I finish my nursery rhyme or eulogy or whatever the "others" or those "others" wish to call it. As usual I get ahead of myself and I need a hand to slow it down. This is now the end of this procedure. Now on with the rest of my experiment.

I'm not using anyone on that wall except for myself.

Except for myself.

Smash all of our technology and pose for a little while, please?

Smash all of our technology and pose for a little while with me, please?

Smash all of our technology and I'll pose for you a little while, please?

Smash all of our technology and pose.

LA VIE EST AILLEURS

128

LAB 2

It's something that's named after a wall. This is my story. Another story. Just my story. A story about several things and scars. Howl. Howling about how everyone goes about their own pace. Never noticing the other lives around us. I howl. I want to meet the all of everyone who makes my smile on my face for real. But distance is safety and safety is insurance and distance doesn't make me feel worthwhile anymore.

Anything that could be turned into a souvenir was taken. I don't want a souvenir, I don't want a timeless face I want to fade into the ordinary. to be accepted as normal. But normality and ordinary are myths and my wounds are real. My wounds are my poems and my poems are my wounds. While supplies last, it's smart money, I'm never really sure it's like the love (or dream) of my life will never be mine. Isolated inside of a face that's half admiring and the other half reluctant to admire. A face that's half soft and half murder.

I hate all the quotes I use. I try to play with them because they make me. Make me, and touch me. I don't try to steal. I've stolen enough as it is, sitting here watching Jim Dean struggle and dance across my screen.

Pick up my pin and I will apologise to you for my crimes. I'm sorry, I don't mean to hurt or embarrass you at the last supper. That's why I write in the dark. I like writing in the dark. I like writing in the half light. I like writing with my raggles. I like writing with myself. Most times I do. I try not to hurt. I try not to do the wrong things. I don't mean to hurt with quotes the quotes I display. I don't mean to hurt. I don't mean to hurt. I display quotes high above my head with pride in the hopes that you can see my breath and feel some of the life I feel when those words paint in front of my eyes.

I love you.

I love all of you.

Please believe me. I don't want to hurt you. Everything now means so much to me as my grandfather's pocket watch ticks and the sun sets. I feel all ugly. I want to love you. Yes, give me the time again Grandpa. I never said I love you. I love you. I love you. I'm scared and I'm cold that I'll make that mistake again.

I love you.

Even when I don't say it. I mean it. I love you all.

I love you all.

I love you.

I would like to explain to you everything. That's cute. No! I don't know why. I keep moving around all the time. From one direction to the another. You're not listening to me. They hurt me. Danger, do not operate. My gnarled up hands are tiring out. It's all right darling, time for supper. Come and eat. I love you. I love you.

Choose your friends, don't let them choose you? Who lives? Everything will rot and divide and fall into none. None of nothing. The flash of my beginning. I don't want to be immortalised, just respected and looked at and smiled at and touched. Do you know what I mean? I'm sure you do. Whether you want to admit it or not. I'm writing for you. Whether you want to admit it or not. You can steal from me if you want, whenever you want. Whether you admit it or not. I just want someone to capture me and hold me and love me, you know, it's happened before. Let's have it happen again. I'm tired, I'd like to change the subject. Again, I'd like to change the subject, again.

I didn't think this would ever come again, I bet you're real good at hanging and purging. You want to see a monkey.

I'm being swallowed whole. Whole. Hole. Look you can see my breath. Here it is with my stomach. Pull that shade down and I don't even realise what I'm writing anymore and I'll just shut down the radio and watch myself get numb and try and wake up in the morning and look at her and them and you and be happy about it all. Be happy about how soft her eyes and hair and lips are and know that it will amount to nothing. Don't call me Plato, I just have to warn him and myself that it's almost time to take the picture of the moon. Goodbye.

The end of the world will come in the middle of the night. Goodbye. It's time to take the picture of the moon. Just like a man going into work and not knowing and not wondering if anything happened at his work while he was gone. Hello moon, hello.

I'm under pressure when I'm fast asleep. That's why there are holes on the inside of my mouth. And to think, I was going to do drugs while writing this.

Come into my tribe. Come into my tribe. You choose. You chose not to give me anything that you read on that wall. I must be a master of the missing chromosomes.

DAMMIT
RAIN ON ME
DAMN YOU

Rain on me, I always expect the worst so I never get hurt or very far up. Sort of the same. Just a fix is all I need, Oh, and get me a Perrier and a fucking motivational tape while you're at it you god damned accountant. Accoutrement be on your accountant. Accoutrement be on your accountant. Buy me up and spit me out like blood and pus from a canker sore. I'll show you how to develop film. You might take these possessions away from me. Not that you haven't already but it's just I'm not sure of anything anymore. Everything is all mixed up, I just don't know anymore. In the morning after my morning physics. After I look at all of my physics maybe I can see you? Hold you? Hold you. I'm not repeating myself to make you feel slow. It's just that I repeat myself to make you feel clear, to help you, so you can (maybe) help me? I'm just not sure anymore. It's never as good as the first time, honest.

More after my negatives and physics and mornings in my little whole hole house hole but it's in me and around me. Do you get it, get this? Get it? Get this? I'm sorry, I'll let you rest.

I apologise because it seems like the only good thing I can do.

She came like a ghost at midnight telling me she was sorry she couldn't give me what I wanted. I felt like dying all over. I felt like I was bad all over. I felt like dying all over. I felt like I was bad all over. I felt and thought she might still be hiding in my home and heart when I finally put this pen down. But I know as soon as morning gently pushes my eyelids open, everything before now and including now will seem like a dream. A dream that I created by wanting too much. I feel ugly and I don't like my "great" things. I'm tired. I'm sorry. I love you. Goodnight, I love you. Goodnight.

Morning. Morning. Morning. I could finish this all right now but I feel that I have a lot of explaining to do. And I'm sure you'd agree with me on that point.

I hate being tested. It interrupts me and I get distracted. Watching people go by and that one female staring at me. She only wants me when she needs my services. She only wants me when she needs my help. And if I need her's she looks at me and says I'm wrong and then starts reading and saying what I just said so it sounds like I didn't help her at all and she just figured it out.

What I'm saying about normality and ordinary is this, it's the acceptable way to steal. The woman I just spoke of is an example of that. She will steal something different from anybody who she deems is different and use it and butcher it and say it was her's all along. Her body is a vice. Smooth in all the places it's supposed to be smooth in. Curves in all the places that are supposed to have curves in. She is a murderer. I...praise and hold up all that was, is and will be different. You can call it stealing if you want to. I guess, in a way it is. But it's just not the way people like her find acceptable because I'm not using. This relates to what I said before about my quotes I take, I don't mean to hurt anyone. She and the rest of her's do mean to hurt. By making me think about resting my lips on her erect nipples, they all know about this user fee. After the thought of kissing and putting my hands on her hips it makes me want to vomit my sex right off my body.

I'm sure you know what I mean, right? Yes. I'm sure you do know what I mean. When I say I want to be touched. When I say I want to be touched for real. Just like the way my grandfather and his watch touched me. I miss his and its gentle but hard way of ticking. It soothed me in an odd way. Know what I mean?

I'm sure you do. You've come all this way already. You've come this far already. So you must be at least partially into my tribe. Come right in. Don't feel nervous, you've heard this all before. Or, maybe you haven't and that's why your eyes keep crossing over this one page of my body like you've known me for years and you like what you see and feel. I thank you for coming this far. Thank you. I don't hate you. Not anyways. I can't hate anyone who has come this far and still looks out and at me for more.

This is, was, left by my bed. Closed. So nothing will escape from me because I need all the friends I can get.

Friends rain.

Friends on, rain on. Me. Friends on me, rain on me. This can and would bring me up. Oh, hello. I know what you're like. You're just like me.

Friends reign.

Friends on, reign on. Me. Friends. Me on friends, reign on friends. Friends on me, reign on me. When the friends are on me and the friends reign themselves, that brings me up and makes me smile and love. And I can figure out all of those important equations and smile and hold out to you. But when the friends just, wait...it's getting mixed up. I'll slow down a bit and show you how I feel.

If friends reign themselves and rains on me I feel lovely. If friends rain on themselves and reign on me it makes me ugly and spiteful and bitter. I'm glad I elaborated. It makes more sense to me. How about you?

The you I mentioned before is just like me sometimes. You reign yourself sometimes (but not often) and rain on yourself most times and try to reign others sometimes. But not often because it's too much work and it makes you tired and down.

Someone I met recently is the lovely I like to give to the most of me and them all. If friends reign themselves most times and rain on yourself sometimes (more often than not) and rain on me (you all others included) sometimes (more often than not) it makes me love and it's very special and natural.

Developing film. Developing myself. Developing yourself. Developing film. Developing yourself. Developing myself. Developing film. Developing our parts. Your's and mine in this film. In this film we all play a certain role. We all play a certain part. We strive to develop our roles and parts in certain ways. Develop yourself and your part and your role. And I'll develop my part and my role. Then together we can develop the whole film. Scale and all. Scale and all of the film. Develop whole scale of the film and we'll all be able to sleep better and rise stronger. Get it? Do you get the whole of my film and picture?

As I write all of this down I am (at least I think I am) developing myself. Take a page from my book (none of that bad stealing, only the nice, caressing, praising stealing) and develop yourself. I told you I'd show you how to develop a film.

Remember what I do when I take a page from someone's book? I make it into that special item that you can look at and it makes all the bad patches go away. I give you permission to steal from me only unless you give it to yourself and everyone in and around you and your radius. And I will do the same.

Pardon me, I'm sorry, I'm not trying to be an empty vessel that just makes noise. I'm not trying to be one of those people who talk a lot but they don't say or mean anything but noise. That sort of person emits his or her usual ejaculations and will never go on to any sort of fame or fortune. Neither will I but you'll go on doing your ego presentation, I'll just go about my business hoping that someone will touch my work and my writings and understand something a little more. Feel something a little more than they did before. That makes me shine and go to sleep a little easier than before.

When that beautiful woman said it was nice to hear me read. I felt like hugging her and thanking her until I could look in my own mirror and look back at her and see in myself that I could read again. I decided to read again. I will read again. Do you hear me? Do you all hear me? I will read again.

Don't stop dressing my wounds. Don't stop dressing my poems. We all twist negatives in a way that makes them more digestible. We all twist them so they can pass right through us. So we can pass right over them. As long as dressing is made for me I know I can crush your negatives.

That's what I thought of last night when I saw that woman who liked to hear me read that other night. Understand? I think you do. We all need to know that when you're at the end of a cliff you can't go backwards because there is too much we regret in our past. We can't go forwards because then we fall to our own cynical deaths. If you can't go backwards or forwards (down) you all have to make a new direction. Up. Go up. Everyone can fly to go up. We all can fly. We all have wings. We just need a little bit of a hand to get that jump. To get that start. We all need a little bit of a hand to get that jump start, before our wings kick in. This all sounds so surreal and tacky, but it's pretty much true. It's just that nobody really wants to admit they need a hand or that they have emotions just like I wrote here. I try to admit it the best I can and hope everyone can pick up on my listings and ramblings. I will read again.

I apologise my dear for repeating myself. I am not repeating myself to make you feel slow. I'm not trying to insult your intelligence. I am not trying to insult you with my apology. I repeat myself to make myself clear to myself. Make sure that I have confidence and understand just what I'm saying and just what I'm getting into. Getting ready to set fires and begin the game again. How about you?

I was crossing a bridge. On my right side it was dark and snowing. On my left side it was bright and sunny. But by the time I had crossed the bridge it was dark and snowing and storming on both sides. I swear this is the truth. I swear to you and myself, this is the truth.

LA VIE ETAIT LA MIENNE

LAB 3

I had this dream about my current English teacher. It was totally dark in my apartment but I just knew it was him. I was letting him read some of my poetry and I had left him in my living room in the darkness to get him some water. When I came back with the whole water jug I started screaming because he had read one of my poems in the pitch blackness of my apartment.

I wish you weren't on my floor. Or even on my physics or chemistry. I feel like grabbing your smooth skinned neck just below your chin and the back of your hair line and smashing your head and mine together. You are a small woman. I am caustic and wish to make peace with you. Female, I wish to smother you in darkness and sand until you show off no more. Your death equals my peace. I wish you to die in my mind. You died a long time ago in my mind, even before I met you, you were dead in my mind.

INTRANSIGENT

I don't trust you. You aren't in my chemistry. She gave me her phone number as an emblem, not as a gift. Get it? Good. I am your subaltern. Sorry if it's not the right word. It's my own volition, throw a sun disc at me and then spend the earth. No, not yet. I'm not myopic or inured yet. No, not yet. Is that what you want? Not yet. No, not yet. Don't tell me it's soft and then leave. Remember, it's something named after a wall.

Look, you can see my breath. No, no, not yet. I'll pull

that sun disk out of my left arm and pay the earth. Pay the earth with that god damned sun disc and my own blood. You give her bile, I give her blood, not much difference, eh? Your eyes keep crossing over this one (these few) page (pages) of my body. If it doesn't get you aroused or me aroused, why get it on? Just get it off. Just get it off. I thank you for coming this far. I thank you for coming. Come. Coming. Came. Gone. Going. Gone. Long gone. Goodbye.

So nothing will escape from me because I need all the friends I can get. And still, some things go somewhere inside me and they just never, ever, come back bout. I hate that. I hate myself for murdering those somethings. It's like my head is too thick (think?) to concentrate. Do you still want to develop film with me? I heard that click again. Does it mean no? Does it mean yes? Does it mean you'll come? Does it mean you'll go? Gone? Came? I know I'm never sure of anyone besides myself.

I hate it when people question my authority because if I question their's, they'd wish me straight to hell. And ever since I saw those ads I've never been able to look or touch jeans or been the same way. Ever again. So let loose the dogs and try and spell order. Can you spell order. Can you spell order? Can you spell order right? Can you spell ordered right? Can't you spell order right? Can't you spell ordered right?

I like to admit to something that I can't identify with. Excuses are not acceptable social behaviour, you know. You know excuses are not acceptable social behaviour. You know. I've never been to the place where my write comes from. It makes me feel like sleeping with my body facing east and my head facing west. And all along she was going around me in a whirlwind. Going in me, like a whirlwind. And those same hands made love to me. Scratch me. Scratched me. Scratch me.

go look in a mirror.
GO LOOK IN A MIRROR!
See?

Sibilant sounds. ˊ That's all. A waste of human potential. She couldn't lift me up high enough. My expectations were too high for myself and her. I guess it's just an experiment in buying and selling. I'm sorry, I'm not trying to degrade you or your image or my image of your image of me or my image of you. But it will always be like seeing used condoms and syringes on a freshly cut lawn in the summer time. I'm just too eager for my own good. And sometimes I feel light sensitive. And those sometimes are the times they close their curtains. Just like the times they are closing their curtains because it gets dark and starts snowing. They are closing their curtains when it gets dark and snows. They have to know snow balls can't be made with water. Especially in the summer time. And it was cold for awhile but it was like watching my favourite hockey team start fighting and it's like, "That's the end of that romance." Damn, I'm not even into sports that much. Damn, I'm not even into romance that much.

Where's that nail? I can't find that nail in the dark. Where's that nail?

Where's that nail? I can't find that nail in the dark. Where's that nail?

I am just too superstitious. I'm just falling my pencil shavings on her phone number and notes that were so special to me. I'm just shedding my pencil shavings on her phone number and notes that were so special to me.

I'LL BE THE THIEF IN THE NIGHT.

AND I'LL SLIT YOUR THROAT.

And in my mind I always see her tossing her head in a sort of bored and frustrated way once she hangs up her phone and I hang up mine. It's sort of a breaking point that makes all the bad patches go away. But not really, because my gums are bleeding. And because my thoughts were that of a murderer's. She was the only one who knew me. I knew, if she was gone, no one else would (ever) know. But I couldn't do it. I just couldn't do it.

Is this linear thinking? Is this thinking in every direction? Is this thinking in lots of directions? I am really trying to hope everyone can pick up on my listings and ramblings because the fires are now ready and the game has begun.

Remember, an experiment. An experiment in buying and selling. That's the key. I want somebody here when I'm not. I want somebody there when I'm not. I now have to get pretty because everyone wants to know what people look like because it says so much about their possibilities. And I am still ugly. But I am still ugly. Get it? Got it. Came. Gone.

Will I ever be pretty?

I hope so.

Because I just couldn't stand

Being four horses with

Two horsemen.

Get it?

Got it.

Came.

Come.

Gone.
Goodbye.

In my target you are. In my room you are. In my mouth you are. I'm never sure if I should drive you out. But I did drive a knife from my insides and it ended up that I did your time and mine. Which is, what is, where is, mine?

Do you have pathos for me? Do I have pathos for you? No. What I have for you starts out as apathy, goes all the way to spite and then pure hatred. Choking the usual back takes only about an hour or so but I crushed that flower and drew a new card. I crushed that flower and drew a new card long ago. You know the flower I'm talking about. It's all those worn out stripped down cliches like, life is a combination of what we are and what we were. Hopefully you won't find many of those bastards on these pages. I'll just go to sleep now. I've had my fill for the day. It's what I should do and we all know that sometimes we just won't do the things we should do. I'm not sure why, maybe it's because most of us are so frightful of standing in a line that we avoid even the things that are good for us. End up being...reticent. Reticence? What is this public reticence anyway? Some sort of fucking banner? And I don't even think I'm anywhere near the halfway point. And I didn't even think I was half way.

And I didn't think I was halfway. And I get so sick of thinking I am nothing. Sick of calling myself nothing. I'm thinking of a famous dream. To try and ease myself. I try not to get angry at your generation for destroying the earth but our race is run and my anger is boiling over. It's hard not to get angry at anything your generation has done. I tore the soft up and put nothing on top to replace it. I've got lots of things to say but most of the time I feel like no one wants to hear it. Or that no one ever wants to hear me. That's why I write. To humiliate and express myself.

The good of the many against the needs of the individuals. I hear words I don't like. Now I know why that man was ripping all those flowers out downtown. It's like what I was saying before. I've (as he had) turned myself into an ass and I might as well go for broke. I mean, this is my diary. It's always better when no one has to think. Especially for himself.

You've read the person. You've seen the book. Now meet the movie. I keep on hearing my name called out by some ghostly female voice. Like she was trying to warn me of an approaching, encroaching forest fire.

Yes. Yes, you can take the covering off of my face. Yes, I will let you take the covering off of my shirt. All things are possible.

I ask too many questions. Why did you come? Then why did you leave? Why did you come again and then leave again?

The people who occupy memory have to be protected from strangers and fingertips and stranger's fingertips. Protected because as the past moves under fingertips parts of the past crumbles to dust. The other parts are turned into those little yellow reminder notes. I'm taking some of the reminder notes down and off of the walls. I have to, because I have to. I feel I have to, can you tell me why? Can you tell me?

It's like you've gone, and it's like all along I was only seeing someone's back and never seeing their face. It's like I was only seeing your back and never, ever saw your face. I hate myself for saying all of this. I hate myself for saying I don't care if you come or not. Or go or not. It's like I've been listening to too many sad songs by The Pogues. Or is it too many angry songs by The Pogues? I don't know anymore. It's like all of my emotions are being fused into one big picture. Some people will always, always make my gums bleed. You're not one of them. It's like all of my great things mean less to me now that you went away. I know now that's a great deal of pressure to put on you. I had to find a way to release that pressure. You had to find a way to release the pressure. But neither yours nor mine worked and I feel like crying. I feel like scarring myself but I can't stand looking at myself because I've scarred myself so badly sometimes before that my arms look all yellow and bruised. And sometimes I hate this puny thing hanging between my legs and eyes. And most times I hate this puny thing hanging between my legs and eyes. Does it have a warning label on it? Does all of this have a warning label on it? No, but that says nothing of the puny thing that I hate. Forget it, just forget it for now. This is just a diary. Just a fucking diary. And I know that tonight I will be woken up to write all of this down.

Don't read this or any of my other writings in the dark because I wrote them that way. And I start noticing small things like the tiny freckle on the bottom of my right foot. And noticing that you can never let other persons know your weaknesses. Except sometimes teachers because they are always discreet. Remember, there are always exceptions to every rule and teachers and special people are the exceptions most times. Because if you can let someone know your weaknesses then they are special. If and only if they don't use them against you. I'm always paranoid about someone using my weaknesses against me. And that's probably why I get such murderous, disgusting thoughts about you. And when I thought that I felt things shatter and it was to the sound of guns. Shattering the room of glass I'm in. So sound off the guns and quit biting the brake pedal and let me escape from my room. The room is in glass and it's my hole.

My room and hole are shattered.

My room and whole are shattered.

And I'm just picking the scraps off of the floor and cutting my hands in the process. I feel as if you never related to me. You never could relate to me. You could never relate to me. And I feel like I just don't want to talk about it anymore. I don't want to talk about it anymore. Again another apology, another sorry, but I am sorry, always. I am always sorry. I am always sorry for how it turned out.

I am always sorry.

I am sorry.

Sorry.

These pages I write on are wet! Why are these pages I write on still wet time after time after all of this time? This isn't linear thinking. Is it? No, I don't think so. I'll sleep on it because it's all vernacular. Just vernacular because I might as well write this in another language because you won't understand most of it anyways. I'm sorry (another one!) if I don't give you enough credit but most times unfortunately, it's true. I sleep on this, these wet pages for awhile because if I keep at it I'll hate what's true and that's nothing new to me. Goodnight.

Maybe that's why the pages are wet, because I had a shower that was too hot. I couldn't get the shower to cool down a bit. Oh well, there is only one way out of here. Oh well, there is only one way out of hear, no, here and that's by sleeping. Goodnight, more later.

A blind man on a galloping horse would be able to tell that I wouldn't send you out into that storm. It's the mind that counts. Attention must be paid. Paid to it. It's involuntary action. Automatism. Insane? Or non-insane? My mind has no more control over my body. What happened? This is a poem that didn't work out. I don't want change. But I do, very badly. This is a poem that didn't work out. This is a poem that didn't work out. But the whole is greater than the sum of the parts. What ever happened to The Replacements and all their songs? Whatever happened to Left Of The Dial, Bastards Of Young and The Ledge?? Whatever happened to them? Things don't work out and I guess things always move on. But I will always be loyal to those who aren't present. Do you know what I mean? I'll never know if you do. I'll never know if I do. This is a poem that didn't work out. Goodnight. I hope I will sleep like a dead one. This is a poem that didn't work out. This is a poem that didn't work out. Goodnight. I'm going to sleep with my past. I'm going to sleep like a dead one. I'm going to sleep with a dead one.

This is a poem that didn't work out.

I can never sleep with my past. I can never sleep like a dead one. I can never sleep like a dead one. I can never sleep with a dead one. Sometimes I'd swear that I hear my typewriter's soft hum but I know that it's been unplugged for awhile. Sometimes, like now, I'd swear I hear the hands of my grandfather's watch moving but the hands didn't move. The hands of my grandfather's watch didn't move today. They just glowed. They didn't move because I hadn't wound it since yesterday. But its ticking sounds louder now and I don't want, can't have, any of the chain attached to it fall through and in between the cracks. I think this is blindness to reality. And I just put it back to where it was and there is only one way out of here. There is only one way out of hear. I'm not sure about it so I'll let you know about it later when I'm a little more sure about it.

This is a poem that didn't work out.

---

knock 'em dead! knock 'em dead corey!
They will kill me with the garbage they throw at me.
when we want your opinion, we'll give it to you.
They will kill me with the garbage they throw at me.
a man who can't handle his tools is not a man.
They will kill you with the garbage they throw at you.
Are any of these thoughts congruent? I'm just edgy because of the heat and low wages. This started before I was born. I wasn't even born yet, but that's no excuse. When I was sixteen someone said to me that I was the oldest sixteen year old on the planet. And I wonder what he would say if he saw me today. I wonder what he would say now that I'm almost twenty two.

Manual handling and knowledge are an act of control. I'm tired of feeling such a weary voice in my head. I'm tired of feeling so old when I'm so young. But it's easier to be older when you're young and younger when you're old. Much easier than it is to be younger when you're young and older when you're old. It's just like a cable sticking right out and then entering back in, but in the wrong place. It's just like being in a boat that had a small leak in it and knowing that the engine is dead and all you can do is sit and wait for the end. It's just like the trees have no rhythm anymore and neither do I. It's just like celebrating your personal life whether you're lost or found or with failure or with success or neither. It's like I didn't know that the light was blinking until I came totally around that pillar. It's just like you turned your back to me and then you turned around and smiled at me and then turned away again. Here comes the snow. It's just like I'm going to put that tripod above my head and above my bed. All along with the first sight of your lips and hair and the back of your neck for as long as I sleep here. For as long as I live here. Here comes the snow.

I am not a mind reader.

They will kill me with the garbage they throw at me.
a man who made peace with his stones.

They will kill me with the garbage they throw at me.
so you're doing nothing but jacking around
with the girls and the little people.

They want to kill me with all of the garbage they throw at me.

as you rise towards your commission,
you are given a good deal more
opportunity to shout back.

They are going to kill me with all this garbage they throw at me.

It's just like I feel like you just stop living once I stop seeing you. Touching you. Being near you. It's just like this is in my mind and I need antibiotics to kill this virus and take it from my skull.

And why don't you relieve yourself on the children while you're at it. And why don't you get me a Perrier and a motivational tape while you're at it.

I am going to die from all of this garbage being thrown at me. I am sorry that all those great Replacement songs had videos, but they were beautifully ambiguous videos that didn't ever destroy my image of these songs. I wish I could be beautifully ambiguous but I think I am feeling funked and nothing is congruent anymore and I want another

148

egg. I want another egg please and the sweater was well made and boredom is a vice. Boredom is a crutch. Boredom from letters and this, this is a poem gone wrong, gone bad, gone sour.

This is a poem that didn't work out. Relax, I want to hear about you and permission. With your permission, why did you give him permission to write it? I want another egg. I want another egg. No webley guns here. I try not to be bored but I feel Jesus is none, nothing and never will be. Just blame it on Dante, but I don't know who he is or was but I'll let you know later if you wish. Yes, I will make it so. Later. My pride and congruency flew gracefully out my glass window long ago. I was just as prepared as you were for those shards of glass to rain down on me. Raining glass shards.

I wrote this on a stone tablet the day Helen Hayes died. My pride and congruency flew out my window. You are just as prepared as I am for not one thing to work out. I should have erased this better. I should never have talked. I should never have opened my mouth. Do you ever feel that way, that you should never have opened your mouth and that you can't even remember the time, the day, the month and the year? I don't feel I can make anyone happy anymore, even myself. Especially myself. Not even myself and I used to be so easy to please. So easy to please. This is a poem gone wrong.

This is a poem that didn't work out because all the garbage they threw at me, just got me funked. And all that garbage got caught in my fingers and I realised I wasn't going to die from it, I just thought I was. This is a friend gone wrong. This is poem gone wrong. I had better just leave it all for now. I'll let you go. When I saw you putting your jacket on in that classroom I wanted to hold you around your waist and beg you to know me. But I am a friend gone wrong. Writing a poem gone wrong.

This is just a poem, gone wrong.

I will let you go now.

But I know my battle will come back after I've pretended to sleep like the dead. I love you, good night. I've gone wrong with a poem and my nose is cold, so cold. Goodnight.

I used to live in my home. Now I just live in a house.

Sometimes I despise being the April fool of intransigence. Intransigence. Intransigent. It's something named after a wall. It's something named on a wall. The wall named it, not me. Can you spell dropping the hot potato? Can you spell order? How about ordered? I never ordered a wall with that sort of name. No, not me. I drop all blame and stand out of the light of your accusing finger. Stand away. Can't you spell ordered right? Can't you spell ordered right away? Can't you spell ordered, stand away? Stand away? Stand away. Stand. Stand in the place where my write comes from because I can't. I've been barred from that venue because of lack of image and knowledge of those ideas. My grandfather couldn't help me with that, my father couldn't help me with this and I can't help myself with that or this.

You know, I said it before, it's an experiment in buying and selling. Buying my ideas from myself and my pen and my typewriter. To get it all out before my feet grow roots and the ideas fall to the ground like the dead useless leaves struggling to the ground in fall. And it starts getting cold for awhile. With all that white darkness fluttering to the ground burying or covering the used, friendly leaves in silent graves. It's not poetic, it's a fact, that you can't hear the last breath of those leaves and it was and is cold for awhile and the summer seems so faraway just like a baby friend who died in your arms last week. You buried him and moved on and the past never feels real again. I envy your strength my friend and I wish you could teach me that sort of innocent intelligence. Then may be I could finally dream about my grandfather and let him to rest. And let myself to rest. Remember? An experiment in buying and selling. And I could never tell which was which when I walked out of that funeral. When I walked out of that church and saw all those quiet people looking so sad. Thinking that when I went in it was dark and almost blizzard-like and that when I came out there was no clouds in the sky. Just like when grandpa and I went walking in the morning. Does this mean something? I can't tell if it means anything to myself or anyone else.

Oh how I wish Soul Asylum could have sung me to sleep in the back seat of my father's car. Sung me to sleep with Black Gold in the almost back of my father's car in the almost front of the funeral procession. But this was three years ago and I am (was) scared that no music that put me to sleep now or then could have put me to sleep then or now. I wish I could see Dave Pirner and ask him if he understands what I'm saying or thinking or why I can't let anything rest when it's including myself. But myself or I or whoever doesn't understand this all so how can I expect anyone else to? I'm sorry for naming all these names. I don't mean to drop them. I don't mean to drop names. I don't know what you mean when you say get on, move on and live strong and on. Help me someone, I've fallen and I can't get up, I've lost all my senses. Don't hold me down, I don't want my instincts to take command. Help me Dave, I've fallen and I can't get up with the music or the writings or the paintings anymore. I'm trying not to be jaded or make anyone feel sorry to me for me. I'm screaming out for help and no acoustics are saving me anymore. No tickets on this train of rain. I'm going away for somewhere for someone and I don't know when I'll be back but I sense that I will come back soon. I love you, back soon I hope, I'll be back soon.

I hope.

In my target you are. In my room you are. In my mouth you are. I'm never sure if I should drive you out or drive you in farther. New mean? New meaning? Knew meaning? Do you know what I'm meaning?

But I hope I did drive a knife from my insides and that I did do your time and mine because then, maybe, I'll know your side of the coin. But which is, what is, where is mine? So many questions questioning the moments of choking all of the usual pathos back because I always feel like all of the sympathy I ask for is unjustified. But I always crush my flowers and new cards long ago. Always. Always, always I hear words I don't like, like calling myself nothing and regret of past generations and always being angry at those words I don't like. That beautiful female voice came onto me last night, warning me of my scars and my past (which could and sometimes are considered to be the same difference), her voice whispered to warn me of my future and that if others make my gums bleed, don't do it to myself.

And her soft furious movements smoothed out the in front of me. Telling, yes her actions seemed to tell me to stop worrying about my puny thing in between my legs. That it is alright to dislike certain things about yourself but choose the correct response to your own morals and criteria. Choose not to hate yourself when there are others around you who love you because it's always debatable who hurts the most, the one who hates himself or the ones who love the one who hates himself.

Goodnight Soul Asylum and Miss Difranco. I love you

all but my hands are all cut up from picking up all the scraps of the floor off of the floor that the blind man on the galloping horse missed. He missed it all and I can't blame him because this is a poem that didn't work out. And indeed, I was loyal to those who weren't present. But he who was on his horse not being able to see the sunset he was riding into was the most loyal of all, I felt. I felt that as strong as I felt that there was only one way out of all of this snow. And that this something had question marks all around it in the borders. No eggs here because I still don't know who Dante was or is or was. And my nose is still so cold from writing these last pages and how I wish that my wish to hold you around your waist and beg to know you would change to simple hug and a kiss from you. And you whispering in my ear that "it's alright, you'll be alright. You won't need to walk around and around in circles looking for a four leaf clover or any clover at all. I am here to hear you and comfort you and hold you, and it will all be alright. I love you, don't leave me hanging or otherwise. Don't leave me at all, I love you. Don't leave me. Don't leave. Don't leave me, I love you."

But there is always doubt in my mind and I wish that I could be sure about something at sometime. But there's a crowd and I have so much more to do with my life that brings on my doubt and I wish I had the time to tell you. How much I want something sure instead of a place that makes me feel so sad inside and I'm using other people's quotes so much. Please Mr. Pirner, don't hold it against me. You're expressing how I feel and I can't make it come out of me alright. All right?

I know this is going to be a shock just like a broken umbrella in a rain storm, thunder and all, but I'll say it anyways. Because I know something you don't know. And

I'm going to tell you that something whether you like it or not. And don't call me kid, either. I'm sick of your reality crushing me.

Something, here's the something.
KEYS,

I lost a bunch of keys in the morning. If you found it or them would you please give me a call. I'll give a reward to you. Thank you very much.

—————————————— LOSER ——————————————

This was written on a wall. This is a poem gone wrong. The meek shall rule the nothing. The meek shall rule the nothing. No more endings in a language I'm not accustomed to. No more. Life was mine and I will grip that short light to feel some pride before this song is done.

THIS IS NO LONGER A REQUIEM.
IT IS A MOTIF.

LAB 4

Remember to break the fixture to make the window fit better. I had a dream that whatever light I turned on in my apartment didn't work and I couldn't move into the kitchen to see if those lights worked because someone was there. And he was plotting my violent death. So I calmly went into my bedroom and laid face down in my bed hoping he would just leave me. He didn't. He jumped onto my bed and crouching over me, he started screaming. Only when I started to wake did he pull away from me. When he was screaming at me I felt like, somehow, smearing some sort of lubricant all over me and hoping that angel Beatrice Dalle would come to my rescue. But no icon of mine could have helped me slip out of that or any other tight situation I got or get myself into.

I turned off the T.V. and took off my clothes because I don't want to think up my pieces of parts of quotes. Don't tear off any material, just listen.

EXCESSIVE
HISTORY
CONTROL
LANGUAGE
IMAGE
SOCIETY
REALITY
DISTORTION
EXTRAPOLATION
CREATION
IMPEDIMENT
INSANITY

HYDROCEPHALIC
AUTOMATION
DRUNKENNESS
DOUBLE JEOPARDY
NECESSITY
ADMINISTRATION
DESTRUCTION
SPIRES

This is now one of Dante's levels. Dante was a prophet, not a writer, a prophet. I am not a prophet. I am not a writer. I am a small doctor. Listening to the prophets and issuing the writers a prescription. I know the cause. I know the cure. I give you the cure on a tiny piece of white paper and leave the choice up to you to obtain the cure for yourself. Remember, here's your notice, your fair notice. There's your fair notice. The choice is yours. To get the cure or to watch me shake my head in dismay as we all rot. Remember, this is not an ego, not a lie. It is truth, it is a fair warning. This is your fair notice. The choice is yours. I leave it all up to you. The choice is yours.

No, no, no. No, not me. I drop all blame and stand out of the light of your accusing finger. I stand away because your non-action is pushing you into your silent grave. A grave no one will hear except yourself. Your problem, not mine. Does any of this mean anything to you? I can understand not wanting to accept my opinions, that's alright. But when you ignore something for the better of our visit...shit.... I just wish you could see what I see. If only you could see what I see with your eyes. We are all just visiting here on this planet. And how can I tip the sun, when it's not mine? How can you tip a son when you forgot who he was. When we all have the same mother what's the point of making up titles? I wish I could write that way. I am a quiet man missing of all titles.

Don't say the title. I don't want to say the title. I don't want you to say the title. Just shh, whisper to me. I need your magic. I need memories with you. There are too many tunnels. I've been through too many tunnels, just whisper to me, because you're the someone who'll get me through the somewhere at the sometime and I really do want to know your side of the coin. I'm under too much pressure and I'm melting into the setting and it's because of my keys and I need to be let out of this burning house. And you, whispering into my ear that "it's alright, you'll be alright." In my dream in my dreams that's you, helping me find the keys. Saying, "You won't need to walk around and around in circles looking for a four leaf clover or any clover at all." And then you hand me the keys and watch me to learn how to use them. And me being your teacher for a brief moment is an influence, or a stimulus prompting me to action. "I am here to hear you and comfort you and hold you, and it will be alright. I love you, don't leave me hanging or otherwise." You understand that the cat that listens and speaks to everyone but me. That cat never talks or talked to me, you hold me back from my bitterness but let me go just enough to escape asphyxiation in that burning house. "Don't leave me at all, I love you. Don't leave me. Don't leave. Don't leave me, I love you." And when we use our team work and we escape into the cool night and the clean air, we turn towards the burning rubble and then back to ourselves in both our eyes. Looking at each other, somebody with a voice with a range like Chris Cornell says just to me, "Why don't you burn it while you still can?" He turns from ourselves and walks off into the night. Because this is all a dream because the keys aren't the motif it's the realism that's the motif. For realistically speaking as beautiful as you are, I can't see you saying the things my dreams tell me you say. And I wish I would because me admitting my doubt is just saying things that stick in my eye. Saying things stuck in my eye. Saying things stuck in my eye. Saying things stuck in my eye.

I'm going for a bloody urine test and it was and is never called execution, it's always called mandatory retirement. And I drank so much water yesterday and today and tomorrow that the test proved negative and my dreams proved positive. But the results of both are just the opposite. The test proved positive and my dreams proved negative. This is the relationship of affection, to try and give them, and myself, a hope for tomorrow. I try my best , the rest is up to you. I tried my best, the rest is up to you. I'm scared that my dreams will cause atrophy of my brain. I'm not sure what to do but hope that all of this motif makes sense to myself when I'm through. And that you will understand why I desperately try to get you to talk to yourself about myself and to get you to talk to myself about yourself. I read all of this on a wall while the sand owl watched in silence waiting for my pride and confidence to come onto me like music from my past that helps me remember good friends and good times. We all need those memories. We all need to know each other's limitations. Yes, I do need memories with you. Yes, I do want memories with you. I just have to understand my limitations and your limitations. Realism. I'd like to let you know this but you're not open late and neither am I. I will hope and wait until our times meet up and that one of us will be together, for even a brief moment, with that other one of us. Can you read this? Can you please read this? I won't have it arranged this time, I'll just hope you'll read it on your own.

I read this on a wall. I read it on a wall.

In a city close to the one that I call home sometimes and other times I call it just a house. I read it on a wall. In a city close to the one where I can call home occasionally a wall spoke to me. And on that wall it said. And on that wall it said this, on several other walls in that city. I have never read this or that or those on any walls in this city. I read most of this and that on walls in that other city and I have never really read any of this on any walls in this city.

I am not blind and I will try not to use any trite phrases or expose any more bromidic expressions. I am not blind nor do I think that in any of my language I am showing off. I am just repeating so you may understand me. If not in one way, then in another way. I just think that if I can't understand myself sometimes then what makes me think you can. I am not blind.

I had better do a painting soon. I had better do my painting soon or I'm going to tear this place I'm living in. To hell with all that macho "sometimes it's better for a man to walk away." I've never considered myself "macho". I've never considered myself a man. Somebody beat it into my head when I was young that a "man" is brave and strong and dominant. I've never thought I was any of those so I've been a bad egg, and nobody wants a bad egg. Nobody wants to buy a bad egg. Has something to do with sports, I think. I hope you don't hold it against me for not considering myself a man. The city's asleep and I wish I was, but I'm sitting here writing to you. The only thing I have left to give to you. I'm not bitter, I'm just tired. Sometimes I'm just not sure what to do. Sometimes doesn't usually apply to this.

I'm not brave enough to explain any of this to you.

I'm not strong enough to explain any of this to you.

I'm not dominant enough to explain any of this to you.

I'm not even sure I'm smart enough to explain this to you because I'm not even sure it's in your language. In a language that I hope you can understand. No more name dropping, except for my own. I'm just as uncertain as the next person. I just want something sure. I just want something sure. But I truly think nothing is sure anymore. I'll stop scribbling for now and let you rest. Rest my friend, rest my love, I'll be here for a little while longer. I'll let you rest my friend, my love, and I'll try to rest myself.

Did you know that in the 1950's in the U.S.S.R. they called assassinations of people whose political beliefs were different "wet affairs"? Interesting, isn't it.

I didn't want her to say her name. I didn't want her to say the other her's name. I just want her to forget about the other hers and the past and it all to go on. I wanted this to go on. I want this to go on longer, not the remorse, just the feelings that come after the remorse.

Go ahead now.

So far as you know, it's more. So far as I know it's less. So far as I know. So far as I choose. So long as I choose. So long as I know, I want her, not the other hers. They mean less to me. Less than she meant to me. And now, the other hers changed in my eyes. Go ahead now, I guess, with much sadness and struggling, I will let you go. I will let you all go. Go ahead now. Go on now. Wait for me later, please?

Sometimes I am kneeling on the mats and I see him staring at me from his timeless photograph. I see Kano Jigori's strong stare and think, "Why am I here, I have no right to be here." At least I try and have fun though. His stare and my Sensei's teachings help me to move on. I need more confidence to relieve myself of the cataract in both of my eyes. My lack of confidence suffocates me. It drowns me in nothingness. It drowns me into nothing. I will learn from this Jigori, I will learn from this Sensei. I promise you both now I will learn from this and move on.

I start noticing little things on myself and little things I do. I start noticing little things on yourself and little things you do. Like when I'm happy how light I feel. Like the tiny, light brown freckle on the bottom of my foot. Like how soft your ear lobes look. Like the way you smile. Even the way you click your pen. I feel like rambling. I feel like I'm rambling. I think it's almost time to bail. I think it's almost time to bail.

Sometimes I feel like baby X, if baby X didn't know who it was or is or will be. Lois Gould, do you know what I mean? If I met you, would you know what I mean? Nagase Kiyoko, would you know what I mean? Your writings speak to me, Lois Gould and Nagase Kiyoko. Even though I haven't read much, your writings speak to me. Sometimes I think I should drop all of the name dropping.
Do you know what I mean?
But when others express expressing expressions that touch me, I want to let all others who touch me, touch them.
Do you know what I mean?

I wish I could write when I'm forced to. But I can't. This says and means and solves nothing.

I will try and take all of my doubt and end it. But I do know, that no one is without some doubt. I understand this and my chosen response is too accept it. I've said it again and I've said this before, I'll try to restrain the name dropping. The dropping of names, I will try to restrain. End. End. End. Fear. Fear. Fear. Mercy. Mercy. Mercy. Nothing. Nothing. Nothing.

SHOW NO FEAR.
SHOW NO MERCY.
SHOW NO NOTHING.
THE END IS NEAR.

My labs are nearly completed, or at least the past three and this one are. You will see a not so grand end is near. But maybe. But maybe. But maybe.

How do you end something like this?

Remorse, remorse. I have no remorse for the rules or the exceptions from the rules. Now do you understand what everyone has taken from me? Leave this. Leave with this? Leave with this. I hate sitting in some place and saying to myself, "Why am I here? What am I doing? Who am I?" This is what the "others" or those "others" or you have taken from me, confidence. Confidence. You stole my pose and confidence from me by smashing your pose instead of smashing technology and pose for a little while, please? Smash all of our technology and pose for a little while, please? Smash all of our technology with me and pose for a little while with me. Won't you please? Technology, normality, ordinary are all described as the bastards of the stealers. Stolen. At least I don't try to steal because I understand that I've stolen enough as it is. I feel so butch. I feel so mean. It didn't bother me, because it's how you cope with what you have. Not how you have what you cope. With. With. With this, his, my grandfather's pocket watch ticking away.

Wishing, just wishing I could ask him what I should do about my past. I'm not even sure he would understand, when even I don't.

I want to talk and touch someone but I feel like an outsider. I don't like looking at this pretty, strong woman in front of me and, believe it or not, I'm writing this for you. I don't mean to be fluffy. I just wish she would come into a tribe with me.

I feel so lonely.

I feel so.

I just need to show, to have a little fix up. I've shown you how to develop film. Touch me and tell me and tell me my repeating is not bad. I'm nice, please leave this room with me? Please leave this room with me. Please.

I'm repeating myself tell me it's not bad, beautiful one, please.

I want to write but I'm too embarrassed to. I'm sorry. Goodbye.

NOTHING

I feel like mutilating myself to an end in this dark. I hate myself. Nothing has changed and nothing will. The noise and the dark. I want to open my skin and bleed all out. Destroy all of my goals. I am a fool. This is not beautiful. It's ugly. I am alone now in all of this noise. I apologise. I still no longer wish to live. I feel I am no longer of any use anymore. My writing pains me while I feel the only good I can do is apologise. Apologise for all of myself and myself and myself.

My eyes always cross over these pages because I can't believe all of this. I shouldn't have come this far.

Thank you. Thank you. I don't hate you. You listened to me and that's as far as you could go. I understand that, I just wish you could go farther but no one is around, how and when I need them. I guess that's just the way things work out. I want to, touch and be touched. Thank you, I don't hate you. I love you.

Nothing ever escapes me because I hold on way too tight. Weigh too tight. Please, I need you, someone, anybody, but my attitude is here. I wear my attitude on my chest and I wish I could cut it off like I did with the scale and all of the developed film. But the mannequins are watching me and I wish all the bad patches would go and leave me. For I am getting bitter and I hate it when I crawl like that. I wish all of the bad patches would go away and you could catch my hope and my listings and pick up on them too. I wish you could catch and pick up on me. Pick me up. But I never could pick myself up. I want to go home and hide from you and never read again. Maybe I should. Maybe I shouldn't. I wish those fires and games had never been set. Maybe you are but I'm not. I'm not sure if it's the right thing to say, I love you. You might be offended. I'm no longer sure if I love you is right, how about you?

Escape. My body wants to escape. I wish to slice myself. Scar myself. You won't buy my book. I am not a writer. I am a nobody. Goodnight. Don't let my attitude bite.

Attitude. Can you blame me or anyone else for having one? My stomach is so upset. Intransigent.

Something that's named after a wall. Can you spell order right? I don't think I ever have been. You'll buy my book. I'm a writer? Who the fuck am I? Spilling all think onto paper. Feeling like I have a hang over, yet I haven't drank anything in two years. You'll buy my book. Who the fuck do you think I am? Who the fuck do you think I am? Should I care? Should you care? Can't you spell ordered right? Can't you? Can't you tell me where my write is from? Because I've never been to the place where my write is from. Can't anyone help me? I know that this hasn't helped me that much. I just always have to remember, it's just an experiment in buying and selling. And you bought it. And you sold it. And I just sold it. I don't think I'll ever be able to buy this myself. I'm too scared to. So I just show my envy of you.

In my target you are. In my room you are. In my mouth you are. I'm never sure if I should drive you out. But I did drive a knife from my insides and it ended up that I did your time and mine. Which is, what is, where is, mine?

Choking all of this usual back I think to myself as much as I want to drive you out. I want to touch you and kiss you and hold you. I want you to touch me and kiss me and hold me too. I'm not sure if I'll ever understand any of this. I'm not sure if I want to or not. I'm not sure if I'll ever understand any of this.

I'm just so cold, please warm me. And it was cold for awhile. And I'd really wish someone would warm me up because I crushed the flower much to my own dismay. And drew a new card much to my dismay. I'm thinking of a famous dream. I'm dreaming of a famous dream. I'm dreaming of my dream. I'm just dreaming of just my dream. I just wish I could warm myself up. I'm so cold. Do you know what I mean? I'm so cold. Do you know what I mean? I'm so cold. Help me. I'm so cold.

We are all out of gasoline because, along with all of the empty shell casings, I exhaled it all out a long time ago. Thinking that they weren't around so that now I'd be a much more sadder person than before. Facts like that sort of rub out all of the words that I don't like. While still letting me know of all of the forest fires that surround me to make my gums bleed all the more. I can forget that puny thing hanging between my legs that I hate. So I can move on and let my hands heal, it's all of those scraps of the floor but it's nothing new to me. Goodnight.

Remember that blind man on a galloping horse? He could explain a lot more of this to you than I could, at least I think he could. I feel like I should be smoking. I feel like I should be living up to your view of what my image should be. Well, living up to or living down to, depending on how you look at it.

I heard a voice whisper to me in the dark, just before I drifted off to sleep, "It shouldn't be hard."

I was very agitated. I was very agitated and I couldn't sleep. Something was crawling all over my body and I didn't know what it was.

Eventually. Eventually, I did sleep, but it was like being in bed with a loaded gun. Eventually, I did sleep though. While sleeping I had a dream. It started out with somebody I know hitting a wall with a baseball bat. I can't remember who it was. But he looked very angry and was hitting the wall very hard. Next I was in bed with Sandra Bernhard. I said to her that I wanted to like myself after someone touched me. She said she could make it so but that she wasn't sure if I really wanted to or not. The next thing I remember is getting closer to the friend hitting the wall with the baseball bat and then going to Sandra Bernhard with her hand on her chest. Then to the friend hitting the wall with the baseball bat. Then back to Sandra Bernhard rubbing my chest. Then back to the friend hitting the wall with the baseball bat. And I eventually woke up because the dream was getting to me. But I do know I will be and always have been and always will be loyal to those who aren't present. All I do know is that this is still a poem that didn't work out and that there is only one way out of here. All I do know is that this is a poem gone wrong and that I hope that the only way out of here comes soon and that I can make this right (write?) somehow. But I was busy trying to do the right thing for so long that I forgot what it was or I lost the idea of the scripture of the right thing along the way.

Whenever I think like this I feel like scratching my face off. Scarring every centimetre, every millimetre of my puny weak body and dying. No more stars in the borders anymore. No more stars at all. Just snow, all of that dry snow. Big dry flakes of snow. The type of snow that makes farmers look towards the future summer with mild fear. A fear of uncertainty. Knowing that this snow will not have any moisture in it. Knowing that their livelihood could melt into nothing in the near future, just like those big dry flakes that are melting even now as we speak.

I wish I could be beautifully ambiguous but I know that it will never be because I am so black and white. No greys. I want some greys. I want another egg. Another egg, so I can have some sort of a rebirth. A rebirth into one of another level of Dante's thoughts because I am so tired of being on the one that I'm on presently.

I feel like I should be smoking or doing something

that you feel I should be doing. No matter how you treat me I still want to hold you around your waist. Thinking that it might stop my nose from being so damn cold. But the only thing that stops me is the light from your accusing finger. Pushing me into your silent grave with you. This is not poetic, it is a fact. This is a poem gone wrong, this is a poem that didn't work out.

Does all of this mean anything to you or me? I can't tell if it means something to myself or anyone else. Rambling around, going away for somewhere, for someone, for something that does mean something to someone, somewhere. Because then, maybe, I'll know your(or anybody else's) side of the coin. But all that usually happens are the ugly dreams, like my friend hitting the wall with a baseball bat, or beautiful dreams, like the one with you whispering in my ear that it's alright, everything will be alright, I love you.

But I usually twist everything because I am to eager to start things or I rush things too much. I always rush things. And I end up losing everything. It's like keeping the frame and throwing away the picture with all the memories still on the photograph.

I'd like to ask you something but I just stare. I'd like to ask you something but I just stare.

Something, here's the something.

KEYS,

I lost a bunch of keys in the morning. If you found it or them would you please give me a call. I'll give a reward to you. Thank you very much.

LOSER.

I'd like to ask you something but I just stare.

I'd like to ask something but I just stare.

I'd like to ask but I just stare.

I'd like to ask but I just stare.

Now do you see why this is no longer a requiem. Now do you see why this is a motif. When we all have the same mother we will no longer say titles. Don't say the title because we all have the same mother. So everyone speaks to everyone. But me. Everyone will speak to everyone and me. Another beautiful dream? Probably, but if he forgot who he was, how can I remember who I am? I am not blind. I had better do a painting soon to prove it. This is the only thing I have left to give to you. The only thing I have left to give to you. In return? What do I want in return? Because everybody wants something in return for something? I just want something sure. I just want something sure. Beliefs, executing different beliefs and calling them, "wet affairs", is disgusting. Don't say I'm a wet affair. I just want something sure. The dream where my last lover changed all in shape and looked even more beautiful and soft than she did before. She whispered to me, "Shh, Shh, it's soft, it's soft." That dream soothed me. It was beautiful. It was sure. It soothed me. And now it's gone. It's gone.

Some beautiful person I know said my writing was beautiful. That I write beautifully. I knew I should thank her. I knew that was right, so I did, I thanked her. But I still feel uncomfortable about her (and your) positive. For I am so used to negative, it's a shock to my system. A system to my shock. Do you still think this meanders? I always meander. Because it seems meandering is more fun than walking straight. But it's the lack of confidence suffocating both of my eyes that makes me uncomfortable when I get positive. Lack of confidence that makes the turns for me meander down, through and around.

It's almost time to bail and I still feel like baby X if it didn't know who it was or is or will be. My response is to accept it. I think it's almost time to bail and my chosen response is to accept it. But maybe.

The end is near but maybe. The end is near but

maybe. I'd like to make you into a servant who has lots to say. A servant for a dictator. I'd like to make you into a servant for a dictator who has lots to say. I'd like to make you into a servant who has lots to say, so you know how I've felt for so long. So you know how I've felt for this long.

This is no longer a requiem, it is a motif. This is (was) a requiem to those who aren't born yet. And I don't want to be in a field full of necrophiliacs when I die. So I make all these twists and turns in a field of necrophiliacs to get out. So I will let thy be done.

So how do you end something? We are all living in the same country but we still make plans because we know they will end. If it's any consolation I don't begin to understand. I have no faith in anyone to remember me or who I am or was or will be. If it's any consolation I don't begin to understand because revolution is just plain over-rated and I don't want any part of it. You've had your fair warning, you've had your fair notice. Now do you see why this is now a motif. Now do you see why I have just left all of the quotes from other names and other names, just a few sentences ago? You all need to know about myself and my prescriptions and now you do know. How about the cure? Well, I'll never even be sure of it so how can I expect you to? So now we're almost done and I hope I have answered some of your questions and left you with even more. Now, here's the big question:

HOW DO YOU END SOMETHING?

You should know by now that I would eventually have to walk away. You should know by now that it's almost time for me to walk away because I don't need more, anymore. I don't need and never needed to be a man, so now it's time to walk away with my motif. So how do you end something? Easy. It's just easy. It's easy.

YOU JUST WALK AWAY.

YOU JUST WALK AWAY.

LAB 5

I'm sorry if you recognise all of my direct quotes. I'm sorry if you are offended by all of my direct quotes. I'm sorry if you hear one of my direct quotes and say to yourself, "That's mine!" You're right, but once it's been exposed to the light it's everyone's. So I won't call it stealing. So I won't call it borrowing. I'll call it....caressing.

Caressing with pride. Relishing its beauty and placing it on a shelf like a trophy. To look at and dream of all those times that are now long gone but were good once they were here. Here and coming in between myself and my loneliness.

How do you end something like this?

Easy, just like this.

You end it.

This not an act of anger, it's an act of charity. It's all so clear now. It's in my head. I want to be clean. I just want to be clean. So don't bother calling me if you're just going to whisper and stare. I'd like to take my life elsewhere because that's where it would be the most welcome. It was named after a wall and that wall has crumbled with the experiment. I can just tell, you won't look at me any different than you did before. I'll meander. I'll meander and I'll go wherever this, or it, takes me. But it would seem that you aren't willing. I know that pain cries have distinct features. I've been screaming all along, but you can't tell if it's pain or not. And....I'm not sure what I'm doing wrong. I must be doing something wrong, because I always do something wrong.

Destruction and mutilation and burning of the synapse. Of the synapsis. Of the synopsis. The means justify the ends. The means justify the ends. The end is what I need.

How do you end something?

Easy, just like this.

You end it.

The end is what I need. The end is the exit and exit is a safe place. And exit is safe because I'll never get there, so it seems.

How do you end it?

Easy, you cut it off.

You end it.

The more I look at this, the more I want to change some of it.

The more I look at this, the more I want to change it.

The more I look at this, the more I want to change.

You just end it.

End it?

Ended.

Dedicated to the memory of:
WILLIAM RONALD HAMILTON
JANUARY 19th, 1915
MARCH 12th, 1990

started this piece on
february 27th, 1993
finished this piece on
april 3rd, 1993
in edmonton